Programming in ANSI Standard C

Gordon Horsington

SIGMA PRESS
Wilmslow, England

Typeset and Designed by Sigma Hi-Tech Services Ltd, Wilmslow, UK

First published in 1991
Sigma Press, 1 South Oak Lane, Wilmslow, Cheshire SK9 6AR, UK

First printed 1991

ISBN: 1-85058-257-2

British Library Cataloguing in Publication Data
A CIP catalogue record for this book is available from the British Library

Printed by: Interprint Ltd, Malta

"Dedicated to Ashley"

Preface

The programming techniques described in this book are implementation independent and all the examples can be compiled on any computer using an ANSI C compiler. If you have a computer, an ANSI C compiler and you want to learn how to program in C then "Programming in ANSI Standard C" is the book you need.

This book has been developed from a tutorial series written for BBC Telesoftware in 1989. The original Telesoftware series was illustrated with programs written in Acornsoft C, a Kernighan and Ritchie version of the C language.

The older Kernighan and Ritchie standard for C has been superseded by the ANSI standard. This book is a complete revision of the original Telesoftware tutorial and focuses on the implementation-independent aspects of programming in ANSI C. The programs in the book have all been compiled with *Acorn ANSI C release 3* using the compiler option *-fussy* to ensure that they comply with the ANSI standard.

Programmers with Acorn Archimedes or Acorn A3000 computers will find this book particulary useful because it contains some specific advice for users of Acorn hardware and software but don't be put off if you don't have an Archimedes or an A3000. The programming techniques you will need to learn are the same whether you use Acorn, Microsoft, Zortech or any other implementation of ANSI C.

This book has been designed to teach programming with worked examples. The examples are very simple and short enough to type in accurately without error. All the example programs can be supplied on an Acorn ADFS 800K 3.5 inch disk or an MS DOS 720K 3.5 inch disk if you send a formatted disk and return postage (international reply coupons if abroad) to the author at the following address:

Gordon Horsington
76, Union Road West
Abergavenny
Gwent NP7 7RH
Wales, UK

Contents

1

Introduction

1.1 In the beginning

The C language has been used to produce many of the application programs that were traditionally written in machine code. A significant number of the word processors, spreadsheets and data bases now in use on 16 and 32 bit micro computers are written in C. The original version of C was conceived for developing the Unix operating system but it has also proved to be a versatile language suitable for a wide variety of applications. It places very few constraints on programmers, it produces fast and reasonably compact programs, and it uses highly portable source code that can be easily transferred from one machine to another.

In 1983 the American National Standards Institute (ANSI) provided a standard specification for C and this standard has become known as ANSI C. The specification has been updated since 1983 and all the techniques described in this book can be used on any implementation of ANSI C which conforms to the latest ANSI C specification. The programs used to illustrate this book have all been compiled using Acorn ANSI C release 3 but, because the programs use implementation independent coding, they can all be compiled with any other ANSI C compiler, for example Microsoft C on an IBM PC, and will execute without any problems.

1.2 Source code, object code and application files

C is not an interpreted language like BASIC. C program code is written with a text editor and stored in a text file. The program code is known as source code and C source code modules (files) have to be compiled into object modules with a program called a compiler. The object modules have to be linked with library modules by another program called a linker to produce an executable file, which is usually known as an application file.

Editing and compiling source code and linking object modules is described in the manual supplied with the language and you should read the sections of the manual concerned with installing the C system as well as editing, compiling and linking before you start programming. This information tends to vary considerably from one version to another and to some extent from one release to the next and it would not be very helpful to duplicate the release dependant information in this book.

1.3 Program structure

ANSI C is a powerful language which can be used to produce well structured programs but, like any other computer language, it is necessary for the programmer to impose this structure on his or her programs. Error checking in the now outdated Kernighan and Ritchie version of C was minimal. In the more modern ANSI implementations it is better but still rudimentary. It is up to the programmer to ensure that the logic and design of every program is correct.

If you have come to programming in C after serving an apprenticeship with BASIC now is the time to forget many of the go-faster techniques of BASIC. Because BASIC is an interpreted language programmers tend to cram as many statements as possible onto one line, to use cryptic one letter variable identifiers and do all they can to make the program file as small as possible. This style of programming is quite inappropriate in C. ANSI C is the programming language used by many professional programmers and the hall mark of a professionally written program is that it should be easy to read and understand with only one statement per line, use meaningful variable and function identifiers and above all exhibit a clear and unambiguous program structure.

Many amateur programmers tend to be very secretive about the program code they write. They often write deliberately abstruse and hard to understand unstructured code in order to protect their ideas. It's as if these programmers believe that it is more important to protect their ideas than it is to write a good program and the end product of all this nonsense is often a program that is not worth protecting at all. If you recognise yourself in this description now is the time to change your ways and adopt the development techniques used by professional programmers.

Programs should be developed using the so called top-down approach. This means dividing the overall objective of the program into logical sections and each logical section is divided into manageable sub-sections, and so on until the sub-sections can be coded as C functions, which are the building blocks of C programs. It is always necessary to plan ahead, to decide how data is to be passed between functions and to use efficient algorithms to solve problems. Failure to adopt these simple strategies will result in poorly designed, unnecessarily complex and badly structured code in any language, including C.

It is possible to identify six stages of program development.

❑ Analysis

❑ Design

❑ Coding

❑ Testing

❑ Documentation

❑ Maintenance

Although these six stages seem to imply a linear process which starts with analysis then moves on to design and so on, in reality the development of most applications involves a considerable amount of backtracking and redesign. The dynamic development process should be systematic and, when necessary, use feedback and backtracking to ensure that the development goals are met. The technique known as structured development is one most likely to meet the goals of any program or system.

Structured development has two important closely related aspects. First of all the system to be developed should be modular and secondly there should be a hierarchical relationship between the modules. The concept of a modular hierarchy can be applied to all the stages of structured program development.

1.3.1 Analysis

It is much more important to analyse and understand a problem and to spend some time designing a program to solve that problem than it is to start coding. Time spent analysing and understanding the requirements for a program and then carefully designing the program before any coding takes place is always time well spent. It is often more difficult to modify the structure of an existing program than it is to start all over again and design a completely new program structure.

One problem you may have encountered if you spent your formative programming years with BASIC is that interpreted languages seem to encourage novices to develop programs at the keyboard without analysing the requirements for the program. The practice of analysing, designing and testing while writing program code is widespread and it can be quite difficult to convince some experienced programmers that it is always a good idea to include and understand all the requirements for a program before writing any code.

Analysis should begin by examining what a program is expected to do. The broad objective should be understood and then broken down into a set of detailed modular objectives. These objectives will include the means of inputting data, the storage and manipulation of information and the outputs from the program. The modular objectives of the analysis should be clearly identified and their relationships with one another understood before beginning to analyse the flow of information within the individual modules. The complete analysis phase should yield a data flow diagram which graphically illustrates the input of data, the transformations of that data, and the output from the program.

Nearly everyone with any formal training in programming will know that schematic data flow diagrams tend to be "written up" after a system has been implemented. For this reason it is probably as well to ignore the formal requirements for flow diagrams and just use whatever diagrams best describe the analysis. Try to include the logical relationships between the modules and the flow of information within and between them.

Program design should only begin when the detailed objectives are clearly understood.

1.3.2 Design

Program design should mirror the top-down approach used for analysis. The design should start with the whole system and proceed to the parts. Top-down design is a process of refinement and subdivision which continues until the subdivisions are small enough to be programmed as complete individual modules which, in the final C program, will be represented by functions. These modules will have clearly defined inputs, a description of the transformations to be used on the inputs and a clearly defined output.

The design of a program starts at the top with the development of the main, or control, program. It then proceeds to the next level with the modules which form the parts of the main objective and then on to the next level and so on until the lowest level of the program is defined. The design should be written out in simple English sentences. Don't start writing program code at this stage but use an English language pseudo-code which describes the way in which the final program code will do its job.

Good programs should be easy to use, predictable, fast and reliable. It is always a good idea to compare your program design with other similar work. If a program is to be menu driven then try to emulate the style of well written menu driven programs. If you are programming on the Acorn Archimedes then always adopt the guidelines for the RISC OS Desktop environment described in the RISC OS Style Guide and choose colours that give suitable grey scales when the program is run on a computer with a monochrome monitor.

1.3.3 Coding

Only after analysis and design should coding begin. Again coding should mirror the top-down approach of analysis and design. Start with the main or control program and then work on the next level in the hierarchy and so on until the lowest level modules are complete.

There are a few rules of structured programming which should be obeyed when programming in C. There is more to structured programming than just obeying these rules but ignoring the rules will almost certainly lead to unstructured programs that are difficult for someone else to understand or debug.

Rule 1

The functions which make up the complete program should be designed and written as independent modules within a hierarchical structure.

Rule 2

Each module should perform only one function and have a single entry point and a single exit point.

Rule 3

Pass data to functions as arguments and return data with arguments or return values. Keep the number of arguments to a minimum and only use global variables when absolutely necessary. It is better to pass a large amount of data to a module with an array than with a number of arguments.

Rule 4

Control the program with if-else, do-while loops, while loops, and for loops.

Rule 5

Never use the goto statement under any circumstances.

Rule 6

Use meaningful identifiers for variables, constants, macros and functions.

1.3.4 Program testing

Testing a program is one of the more difficult phases of program development. There is a tendency to assume that if a problem is sufficiently well analysed and the program is properly designed and carefully coded then testing is fairly straight forward. For anything other than trivial programs this can be far from the truth and it can be virtually impossible to fully test a complex program by executing all the program modules in sequence. If exhaustive testing is not possible then it is important to recognize the limitations of non-exhaustive testing. Non-exhaustive testing may reveal the presence of an error, but it cannot reveal the absence of one. Even fixing the known bugs in a program can in turn create new bugs.

When exhaustive testing of a program is impractical or impossible the two most commonly used strategies for testing are bottom-up and top-down non-exhaustive testing.

Bottom-up non-exhaustive testing

Bottom-up testing of programs involves individually testing each module of the program, then testing groups of modules and finally testing the complete program. As its name suggests this is the reverse of the procedures used in the top-down process and it is the preferred method for testing relatively small programs. This method is very effective at quickly finding errors within the individual modules of a program but less effective at detecting problems with the interaction of modules in complex programs.

Top-down non-exhaustive testing

The interaction between modules can be tested before the individual modules are tested. This is known as top-down testing. The first step involves modifying and simplifying the modules so that the highest level of a program can be tested without any interaction between the lower level modules. When the main routine has been verified then the lower level modules can be modified to start accepting data. Appropriate test runs can then be made again. This process continues until the complete program is tested. Top-down testing mirrors the work involved in top-down design.

Which ever method of testing is adopted it is necessary to give careful thought to the data to be used for the test. It is often useful to input out-of-range values or unexpected data to test the ability of a program to cope with these situations.

Novice programmers often make two fundamental mistakes during program development. First of all they start to write program code before a problem has been analysed or designed. This tendency to analyse and design while coding can prolong the development time of even a simple program and can make the completion of a complex program virtually impossible. The second mistake is to fail to test the program effectively. It is not good enough to ask one of your friends to run the program to see if it's OK. You should test the program systematically using one of the methods described above.

1.3.5 Documentation

A well designed program can be self documenting. If you use meaningful variable identifiers and sensible comment lines within each module then it should be possible to come back to the program in six months time and easily understand what it was designed to do. The analysis and design phases will also provide information for writing up a complete documentation of the program. Documentation should be done at every stage of program development and not left until everything else has been finished.

1.3.6 Maintenance

The last stage of program implementation is program maintenance. A trivial program will probably never need any maintenance but large programs often go through many editions as bugs are found and removed and new requirements are added to the original program. If program maintenance is to be successful then modular program design and full documentation are vital. Programs must be designed with maintenance in mind and you must not assume that because you understand why a program works when you write it that you will still understand why it does what it does when the time comes to modify the program. Remember that if you have difficulty understanding your own programs then it will be quite difficult or even impossible for someone else to maintain them for you. All good programs are easy to understand and maintain. Cryptic coding is evidence of bad design and unprofessional programming.

2

Comparing BASIC to C

2.1 Very simple programs

This chapter will introduce some of the basic concepts of programming in ANSI C by comparing some very simple programs written in BASIC to equally simple programs written in C. In later chapters only C source code will be used to illustrate the programming techniques.

The most simple BASIC program I can think of is

```
10 END
```

this program just stops as soon as it starts running. An equivalent ANSI C source code program is

```
#include <stdlib.h>

int main(void)
  {
  exit(0);
  }
```

This source code is case sensitive and has to be written with a text editor, saved to disk, compiled and linked with the C library modules to produce an executable application file. The C source code does not use line numbers and so the program can be laid out as required. We can write the entire program on one line if we choose to do so, for example

```
#include <stdlib.h> int main(void) { exit(0); }
```

C programs are much easier to read if we restrict them to one statement per line. There is nothing to be gained by cramming multiple statements onto one line like this because the size of the executable code will be independent of the formatting of the source code.

There are very few constraints on the layout of C source code but it is a good idea to arrange the source code in such a way that is easy to read and understand. This usually means typing just one statement per line. It also helps to identify blocks of code if the source code is indented two spaces after every opening brace { and the indent is reduced two spaces after every closing brace }.

Functions are the building blocks of C programs and they take the place of the main program, as well as the functions, procedures and subroutines used by BASIC. The body of a function consists of statements constructed from keywords, function calls, and expressions formed from operators and their operands. The statements are usually terminated with a semicolon unless the statement is normally followed by an opening brace. Braces are used to group statements within a function into blocks of code.

A program can use any number of functions but every program must have one, and only one, function called main. The above program defines the function main which calls another function called exit. The function exit is defined in the file stdlib.h. The file stdlib.h is the ANSI general purpose header file and it is included in the program with the statement

```
#include <stdlib.h>
```

Almost every C program includes header files in this way. The two most commonly used header files are stdio.h and stdlib.h, the standard input and output header file and the general purpose header file respectively. #include is one of many preprocessor directives which are used to create commands for the preprocessor phase of compilation. Preprocessor directives always begin with the hash symbol # and preprocessor commands never end with a semicolon because they are not C statements. They are commands to the compiler which are dealt with before any translation of the source code into object code takes place.

Every C program has a function called main which is the equivalent of a BASIC main program. In the program above the definition of the function main starts with

```
int main(void)
```

The keyword int is used to inform the compiler that the function main will return an integer value. The function main always returns an integer value. The identifier of the function is followed by parentheses ( ) which enclose a list of any parameters passed to the function or the keyword void if no parameters are used.

The braces { } which follow the first line of the definition of the function main enclose the body of the function. One function can call other functions and in this example the function main calls the function exit which is used to return control to the operating system. The argument 0 is passed to the function exit and this zero argument is used to indicate exit success or completing the program without any problems.

Notice that the first line of the function main is not terminated with a semicolon but the call to the function exit is followed with a semicolon. In general, statements within braces are terminated with a semicolon. There are exceptions to this rule and statements within braces which are normally followed by an opening brace are not terminated with a semicolon.

If we replace END in the simple BASIC program above with STOP and then run the program, the BASIC interpreter will respond with

```
Stopped at line 10
```

In C, we can use the exit function to give some information about the conditions under which a program halts by passing a non-zero argument to exit. This use of the exit function can be demonstrated by compiling, linking and executing the program exit. There are two symbolic constants defined in the header file stdlib.h called EXIT_SUCCESS and EXIT_FAILURE. The symbolic constant EXIT_SUCCESS is equivalent to integer 0 while EXIT_FAILURE is equivalent to integer 1. Using the function call

```
exit(EXIT_FAILURE);
```

is exactly the same as using

```
exit(1);
```

and both return control to the operating system indicating an unsuccessful program termination. You should always return control from a program to the operating system with the function exit. Use

```
exit(EXIT_SUCCESS);
```

if the program terminates successfully and

```
exit(EXIT_FAILURE);
```

if the program terminates under an error condition. The function exit will close all open files, remove any temporary files and return the status indicated by the argument passed to exit.

```
/*
 * file name: exit
 * demonstrate the use of the exit function
 */

#include <stdlib.h>

int main(void)
  {
  exit(EXIT_FAILURE);
  }
```

The effect of running the program exit varies from one computer to another. The ANSI standard does not specify how the operating system should respond to an exit failure but a typical response to an exit failure is for the computer to return control to the operating system and to display

```
Exit(1)
```

On the Acorn Archimedes the exit status is used to set the value of Sys$ReturnCode. An exit failure will assign the value 1 to Sys$ReturnCode. To display the current value of Sys$ReturnCode press f12 to enter the command line mode and then type

```
show Sys$ReturnCode
```

The operating system will respond with

```
Sys$ReturnCode : 1
```

The effect of an exit failure is certainly not the same as BASIC reporting the line number of the STOP command but it can be used in a similar way to indicate the error conditions under which a program halts. The following program can be used to enter any integer in the range from 0 to 255 to demonstrate the effect of changing the value of the argument passed to exit. On the Acorn Archimedes the value of the exit status is always used to assign a value to Sys$ReturnCode.

```
/*
 * file name: status
 * try new values for exit status
 */

#include <stdio.h>
#include <stdlib.h>

int main(void)
```

```
{
char status[10];

puts("Enter exit status");
exit(atoi(gets(status)));
}
```

The programs exit and status illustrate the use of comments enclosed within the symbols /* and */. Comments can extend over more than one line, as shown in these programs, or we can begin every line of a comment with /* and end every line of a comment with */ if we choose to do so. Comments cannot be nested and the first of the following comments is illegal.

```
/*
/* illegal use of nested comments */
 */

/*
 * legal use of comments
 */
```

Comments are always ignored by the compiler. Spaces, tabs and new lines are used to separate the components of the source code and, in general, they are also ignored by the compiler. The most important separator in C is the semicolon which is used to indicate the end of a statement. The only time a new line is essential is after the very last line of code in a module and you will see in chapter three that the use of space characters is restricted in macro definitions. Spaces, tabs and empty lines are referred to as white space separators and the white space outside functions is known as the global white space.

2.2 for loops

The next BASIC program is a slightly more interesting candidate for conversion into C because it actually does something useful by calculating the factorials of the numbers 1 to 5.

```
10 REM basloop1
20 factorial% = 1
30 FOR pass% = 1 TO 5
40   factorial% = factorial% * pass%
50   PRINT pass%;" factorial = ";factorial%
60 NEXT
70 END
```

This BASIC program is converted into the C program forloop.

```
/*
 * file name: forloop
 * convert the BASIC program basloop1 into C
 */

#include <stdio.h>
#include <stdlib.h>

int main(void)
  {
  int factorial;
  int pass;

  factorial = 1;
  for (pass = 1; pass <= 5; pass++)
    {
    factorial *= pass;
    printf("%d factorial = %d\n", pass, factorial);
    }
  exit(EXIT_SUCCESS);
  }
```

The for loop in BASIC is controlled by the FOR statement and loops from the line after the FOR statement to the NEXT statement. The for loop in C is controlled by the for statement and loops from the opening brace after the for statement to the corresponding closing brace.

The program forloop calls two functions, printf and exit. The function printf, which displays the result of the calculation, is made available to the program by including the header file stdio.h and the function exit is made available by including the header file stdlib.h. The preprocessor commands

```
#include <stdio.h>
#include <stdlib.h>
```

use the preprocessor directive #include to include the files stdio.h and stdlib.h into the source code so that the contents of these files becomes available to the program as if the contents were written in the source code where the #include commands are positioned.

The types and identifiers of variables have to be declared in C before they can be used. This is common to most compiled languages but quite unlike BASIC which provides a new variable whenever an unrecognised variable identifier, or even a spelling mistake, appears. The variables factorial and pass are declared in the program forloop as type int, which is a 32 bit integer. There are a number of other data types which can be used in programs. These include char (character), float (single precision floating point) and double (double precision floating point).

Declaring a variable reserves memory for the data associated with the variable identifier and ensures that the correct operations are used to manipulate the data. C compilers are optimised to use type int for integers and type double for floating point numbers. Data items can be made global (available to any function) by being declared in the global white space outside functions, or local to a particular function by being declared within that function. The integer variables factorial and pass are local to the function main.

The for loop in the program forloop uses the integer variable pass as a control variable and the initial value of pass is 1. The statements within the braces which follow the for statement are executed while the variable pass is less than or equal to 5 and the variable pass is incremented by 1 with every loop. The braces and statements which form the body of the for loop have been indented to make it clear that they are a distinct block of code.

The statement

```
factorial *= pass;
```

uses one of the many special assignment operators available in C and it is equivalent to the C statement

```
factorial = factorial * pass;
```

Although these statements are equivalent, almost every experienced C programmer would choose the special assignment operator *= because it produces a more efficient, faster running program.

The function printf displays the result of the calculation with every loop. The text within quotes in the printf function call is known as a control string and it is used to describe the format of the text and the list of variables to be displayed by printf. The conversion specifier %d in the function call

```
printf("%d factorial = %d\n", pass, factorial);
```

is used to indicate that the variables pass and factorial are to be printed in denary (base 10) integer format. Conversion specifiers which control the format in which variables are displayed always start with the % symbol. Other commonly used conversion specifiers are %c for single characters, %s for character strings, and %f for floating point numbers.

The \n in the control string is an escape sequence which indicates that the new line character is to be printed at the end of the formatted text string.

The printf function call can be read as "print the integer pass in denary integer format followed by the character string " factorial = ", followed by the integer factorial in denary integer format and then print a new line character". The following output is produced by the program

```
1 factorial = 1
2 factorial = 2
3 factorial = 6
4 factorial = 24
5 factorial = 120
```

2.3 do-while and while loops

The REPEAT-UNTIL loop in BASIC has no direct counterpart in C but the logically opposite looping construction known as a do-while loop is available. REPEAT-UNTIL and do-while are logically opposite because the former loops until a conditional expression is true and the latter loops until a conditional expression is false, which is the same as while a conditional expression is true. The BASIC program basloop1 can be modified to use a REPEAT-UNTIL loop as shown in the program until. The program until is converted into the C program doloop.

```
10 REM until
20 factorial% = 1
30 pass% = 1
40 REPEAT
50   factorial% = factorial% * pass%
60   PRINT pass%;" factorial = ";factorial%
70   pass% = pass% + 1
80 UNTIL pass% > 5
90 END

/*
 * file name: doloop
 * convert the BASIC program repeat into C
 */

#include <stdio.h>
#include <stdlib.h>
```

```
int main(void)
  {
  int factorial = 1;
  int pass = 1;

  do
    {
    factorial *= pass;
    printf("%d factorial = %d\n", pass, factorial);
    pass++;
    }
  while (pass <= 5);
  exit(EXIT_SUCCESS);
  }
```

The program doloop declares two integer variables identified as factorial and pass and initialises them at the same time. The program also uses another special assignment operator in the C statement

```
pass++;
```

This statement is equivalent to the C statement

```
pass = pass + 1;
```

and both of the above statements are equivalent to the BASIC statement

```
pass% = pass% + 1
```

The do-while loop demonstrated in the program doloop always executes the statements within braces at least once before the conditional expression associated with the keyword while has the opportunity to halt the loop. There is another looping construction available in C which evaluates a conditional expression before every loop. This is known as a while loop and the program doloop can be rewritten as the program whileloop. Notice that the conditional expression

```
(pass <= 5)
```

following the keyword while in the program whileloop is not terminated with a semicolon but the same conditional expression in the program doloop is terminated with a semicolon. This is an example of the rule that statements within braces which are normally followed by an opening brace are not terminated with a semicolon.

```
/*
 * file name: whileloop
 * convert the BASIC program basloop2 into C
 */

#include <stdio.h>
#include <stdlib.h>

int main(void)
  {
  int factorial = 1;
  int pass = 1;

  while (pass <= 5)
    {
    factorial *= pass;
    printf("%d factorial = %d\n", pass, factorial);
    pass++;
    }
  exit(EXIT_SUCCESS);
  }
```

2.4 Conditional expressions

Conditional expressions are used in BASIC in the IF-ELSE construction. The simple program basicif can be converted into the C program cif.

```
10 REM basicif
20 cardinal% = 1
30 IF cardinal% = 1 THEN
40   PRINT"cardinal = 1"
50 ELSE
60   PRINT"cardinal not = 1":STOP
70 ENDIF
80 END

/*
 * file name: cif
 * demonstrate if-else
 */

#include <stdio.h>
#include <stdlib.h>
```

```
int main(void)
  {
  int cardinal = 1;

  if (cardinal == 1)
    {
    puts("cardinal = 1");
    }
  else
    {
    puts("cardinal not = 1");
    exit(EXIT_FAILURE);
    }
  exit(EXIT_SUCCESS);
  }
```

Notice that C uses == to mean "is equal to" in the condition expression following the keyword if. Using the if-else construction is not the only way to convert the BASIC program basicif into C. There is another construction known as switch-case which can be used when a conditional expression evaluates to give either an integer or a character result. The switch-case construction can be used to convert both simple IF-ELSE conditional statements and more complicated chained IF-ELSE statements. The program cif can be rewritten as the program case.

```
/*
 * file name: case
 * demonstrate switch-case
 */

#include <stdio.h>
#include <stdlib.h>

int main(void)
  {
  int cardinal = 1;

  switch (cardinal)
    {
    case 1:
      {
      puts("cardinal = 1");
      break;
      }
```

```
    default:
      {
      puts("cardinal not = 1");
      exit(EXIT_FAILURE);
      }
    }
  exit(EXIT_SUCCESS);
  }
```

The expression following the keyword switch is evaluated and if the result of the evaluation is 1 then the statements in braces after the label case 1: are executed. If the expression does not give the result 1 then the statements in braces after the label default: are executed. The keyword break is used to break out of the switch-case list of cases as soon as the appropriate case has been found and required statements have been executed. There can be any number of case labels, such as case 1: case 2: case 3: and so on, used to construct the equivalent of chained IF-ELSE statements.

2.5 goto

Adopting a structured approach to programming is very important and, because of this, it is as well to ignore the C equivalent of the BASIC statement GOTO. Most high level languages implement a goto statement and C is no exception. The use of goto statements seems to encourage the most appalling unstructured programming style. There is never a need to use goto but, if you feel that such rules are made to be broken, then the following BASIC program can be converted into the C program Cgoto.

```
10 REM basicgoto
20 PRINT "Endless loop"
30 GOTO 20


/*
 * file name: Cgoto
 * demonstrate the goto statement
 */

#include <stdio.h>

int main(void)
  {
  again:
  puts("Endless loop");
```

```
goto again;
}
```

The label again: is an identifier which must appear somewhere in the same function as the goto statement. Labels must be followed by a colon and not a semicolon. The function puts is another function from the stdio.h header file and it is used to output simple, or unformatted, character strings to the screen.

2.6 Program modules

BASIC program modules are coded as either functions, procedures or subroutines which are called from the main program or from other functions, procedures and subroutines. In C all modules are coded as functions. There are no procedures or subroutines.

The BASIC program basicabs uses a function to determine the absolute value of a number and this program is converted into the C program Cabs.

```
10 REM basabs
20 cardinal% = -10
30 cardinal% = FNabsolute(cardinal%)
40 PRINT"absolute value of -10 is ";cardinal%
50 END

60 DEFFNabsolute(ordinal%)
70 IF ordinal% < 0 THEN ordinal% = -ordinal%
80 =ordinal%


/*
 * file name: Cabs
 * user defined function
 */

#include <stdio.h>
#include <stdlib.h>

int main(void)
  {
  int absolute(int ordinal);
  int cardinal = -10;

  cardinal = absolute(cardinal);
```

```
   printf("absolute value of -10 is %d", cardinal);
   exit(EXIT_SUCCESS);
   }
int absolute(int ordinal)
   {
   if (ordinal < 0) ordinal = -ordinal;
   return ordinal;
   }
```

The program Cabs demonstrates the use of function prototypes. The function prototype is the statement

```
   int absolute(int ordinal);
```

following the opening brace of the function main. This statement does not call the function absolute. The prototype is used to declare the function in the same way that variables are declared. Function prototypes declare the value returned by the function, in this case the function absolute returns the data type int. The prototype is also used to declare the types of the parameters received by the function, in this case the integer ordinal. Prototyping is used to facilitate error checking.

The function main passes the argument cardinal to the function absolute where it is accepted as the parameter ordinal. Passing an argument and receiving it as parameter in this way makes the variable ordinal local to the function absolute.

The keyword return is used to return the absolute value of ordinal to the calling function main where the returned value is assigned to the variable cardinal.

2.7 Programming in C

ANSI C is a much more powerful programming language than BASIC and sooner or later you will want to give up the idea of converting BASIC programs into C and start programming purely in C. When you become proficient in C you will probably neither want to nor need to go back to BASIC.

C source code modules (files) contain comments, preprocessor commands, global declarations, and functions. The functions, in turn, contain local declarations, comments and executable statements. Executable statements are built up from identifiers (variable and function names), keywords, constants, character strings, operators and separators.

Variables and functions are identified by suitable names which should suggest their purpose. For example, the function absolute in the program Cabs was used to determine the absolute value of the integer variable cardinal. These identifiers must begin with either a letter or an underscore and can contain any alpha-numeric characters or the underscore. The first 31 characters of identifiers are significant. The following are C keywords and these must not be used as identifiers.

Keywords used to affect the flow of control in a program

Keyword	*Meaning*
break	used to escape from a loop or a switch statement
case	used in the switch-case construction
continue	branch to the start of a loop from within that loop
default	used in switch-case construction
do	statement at the beginning of a do-while loop
else	the second option in an if-else statement
entry	reserved for future use
for	used to control a loop
goto	go to a label
if	used in a conditional statement, often with else
return	return a value from a function to its calling function
sizeof	return the size of a data item in bytes
switch	used to form a multiple conditional statement
while	used to control while loops and do-while loops

Keywords used as part of a declaration

Keyword	*Meaning*
auto	automatic storage class
char	character type
const	fixed or constant data
double	double precision floating point type
enum	enumerated data
extern	external storage class
float	single precision floating point type
int	integer type
long	long integer type
register	register type
short	short integer type
signed	type prefix to indicate signed data
static	static storage class
struct	structure type
typedef	statement used to rename a type
union	union type
unsigned	type prefix to indicate unsigned data
void	void type
volatile	prefix for variables that can be altered outside program control

These lists of keywords are extended with every header file included in a program. Including stdio.h adds keywords such as FILE, stdin and stdout to the list and stdlib.h adds keywords such as EXIT_SUCCESS and EXIT_FAILURE. Header files are used to define functions and macro instructions and we must not use the function and macro identifiers defined in the header files as names for our own identifiers. It is necessary to be very careful when choosing the names for the identifiers of variables and functions.

2.8 Passing arguments to main

We can pass arguments to the function main just as arguments can be passed to any other function. Any number of arguments can be made available to a program by specifying two parameters in the main function definition. By convention these parameters are called argc and argv and, if we want to use them, the first line of the main function definition has to be typed as

```
int main(int argc, char *argv[])
```

The first parameter, argc, is an integer which stores the number of arguments passed to main and the second, argv, is an array of pointers which point to the arguments.

Arrays are used in C, as in most high level languages, to group a number of variables under a single array identifier. Square brackets are used with arrays and the elements of a three element array defined as list[3] are referred to as list[0], list[1] and list[2]. Pointers are a special type of variable which store the addresses of other data items such as variables or functions. The reserved word * is used in front of a variable identifier to declare the variable as a pointer.

If a C program is executed by typing the application file name followed by any number of arguments then the variable argc will store the number of arguments plus 1 and the char array argv will contain a set of pointers to the application file name and the list of arguments typed after the file name. If an application file name is followed by two arguments then the variable argc will be assigned the value 3 and there will be three pointers, argv[0], argc[1] and argv[2], pointing to the application file name, the first and the second arguments respectively.

If, for example, we want to pass the values 1.2 and 2.4 to a program called numbers then we can do so by typing

```
numbers 1.2 2.4
```

The array argv stores a set of pointers to the list of words typed after the command line prompt and not a set of pointers to the list of arguments. The pointer argv[0], which is known as the zeroth pointer, always points to the application file name and not to the first argument. The first argument is pointed to by argv[1], the second argument is pointed to by argv[2], and so on.

The arguments are typed as character strings after the application file name and they are made available to the executing program by pointers to these character strings. C does not make any attempt to interpret numeric strings as integers or floating point numbers – it is up to the programmer to convert the character strings into the appropriate type of data if this is required. The functions which provide the conversion operations are defined in the header file stdlib.h which must be included in the program if they are required. The two most useful conversion operations are ASCII to floating point and ASCII to integer. These operations are performed by the functions atof and atoi respectively.

The program arglist can be used to read any number of arguments after the application file name and an attempt is made to convert each argument into both a floating point number and an integer. Compile and link the program, enter the command line mode and type, for example

```
arglist first second 1.23 4
```

The program will respond by displaying every argument as a string of characters and also the result of using atof and atoi in an attempt to convert the arguments into floating point numbers and integers.

```
/*
 * file name: arglist
 * read arguments following the program name
 */

#include <stdio.h>
#include <stdlib.h>

int main (int argc, char *argv[])
   {
   int pass, result;
   double answer;

   printf("argc = %d\n\n", argc);
   for (pass = 1; pass < argc; pass++)
      {
      printf("argument %d = %s, ", pass, argv[pass]);
```

```
      printf("double: %f, ", answer);
      result = atoi(argv[pass]);
      printf("integer: %d\n", result);
      }

  exit(EXIT_SUCCESS);
  }
```

Using arguments passed to the function main is a convenient way of making data available to a program but it does conflict with the preferred method of running programs from the Desktop which involves double clicking on the application file icon. Whenever arguments are passed to main in the example programs in this book an alternative form of input which is compatible with the Desktop will also be made available. This involves some extra coding but it makes the program easier to use and more flexible.

2.9 Obey files and Batch files

A simple way of passing arguments to a program while still using the double clicking method of running the program is to create an obey file with a text editor, store the obey file on disk, and then double click on the obey icon. Obey files are the Archimedes RISC OS equivalent of the more familiar batch files.

To create a suitable obey file on the Archimedes first of all load Edit and then click Menu on the Edit icon on the icon bar. This produces a menu with the options info, create and quit. Create leads to a sub-menu which will allow you to open a window for a number of different file types including obey files. Select the obey file option and then type, for example

```
 arglist first second 1.23 4
```

You can, if necessary, include the full path name in this command rather than just the simple file name. Press Return after the last character in the command and save the text in the same directory as the application file created from arglist. You can now double click on the obey file icon and pass the list of arguments from the obey file to the program.

Edit is a very useful program to use with C and I recommend reading the section on Edit task windows in the RISC OS User Guide. Edit provides a very simple way of creating new task windows and running your C programs in a multi-tasking environment.

3

The preprocessor

3.1 The preprocessor phase

The C compiler has a preprocessor phase which occurs before compilation. The preprocessor can be used to include files within a program, to define, test and undefine macro instructions (macros), and to debug programs.

The preprocessor uses directives which are prefixed with the hash symbol. These directives are used to construct preprocessor statements or commands some of which, such as #if, #endif and #error, can be used both inside and outside the body of functions while others, such as #include, #define and #undef can only be used in the global white space outside functions.

The following preprocessor directives are available to ANSI C compilers.

Directive	Meaning
#include	include a file
#define	define a macro
#undef	"undefine" an existing macro
#if	test an expression
#if defined	test to see if a macro has been defined
#if !defined	test to see if a macro has not been defined
#else	optional with #if
#elif	a combination of #else and #if
#endif	always associated with #if
#error	used in debugging
#line	used in debugging
#	string generation
##	concatenation
#pragma	system dependent statements

3.2 #include

The #include directive will be used in almost every C program to include files such as the standard input and output header file, stdio.h, and the general purpose header file, stdlib.h. Include statements are usually placed in the global white space at the top of the source code. The files included in programs are usually a special type of file known as header files which are identified by the suffix .h, although any text file can be included in a program.

Including header files extends the list of reserved words, macros and functions available to a program and it is hard to imagine any useful C program that does not include the header file stdio.h to provide input and output functions. When a file is included in a program all the macros and functions defined in that file become available to the rest of the program. Some versions of C automatically include header files without the programmer having to use #include statements in the source code but this is not the usual practice and you should not assume that any header files are automatically included.

The preprocessor statements in the following outline program instruct the preprocessor to include the files stdio.h, stdlib.h and myfile.h so that the contents of these files become a part of the program file being compiled.

```
#include <stdio.h>
#include <stdlib.h>
#include "myheader.h"

int main(void)
   {
   /* statements */
   }
```

When a file name is enclosed within angled brackets the preprocessor searches for the file in the general include directory which, for Acorn ANSI C, is within the compiler itself. If the file is not found then the preprocessor searches the system path.

If a file name is enclosed within quotes the preprocessor searches for the file in the same directory as the source code file and if the file is not found there then the preprocessor searches the system path. Searching for include files is both an operating system and a filing system dependent activity and you should refer to your compiler manual for more information but, as a general rule, all the standard ANSI C header files should be included in angled brackets and all the user-defined header files should be included in quotes and stored in sub-directory h of the work directory (Acorn ANSI C and Beebug C). The header file myheader.h is stored by the Acorn

ADFS as the file myheader in sub-directory h, not as the file myheader.h which, in the Acorn ADFS, is file h in sub-directory myheader. If you use MS DOS just store your user-defined header files with the suffix .h in the same directory as your source code files.

The following header files make up the standard ANSI library (also known as the standard C library) and they are available to all ANSI C compilers. This library provides all the standard facilities of the language as defined in the ANSI standard document. Source code which only uses the standard ANSI library will be portable to other environments if an ANSI library is available for that environment. Only the ANSI library will be used for header files in the programs used to illustrate this book.

<assert.h>	puts diagnostics into programs
<ctype.h>	functions for testing and mapping characters
<errno.h>	definition of error conditions
<float.h>	limits of floating point computations
<limits.h>	limits of integral objects
<locale.h>	national characteristics for day-month-year
<math.h>	22 mathematical functions
<setjmp.h>	bypass normal function call and return
<signal.h>	handling conditions reported during program execution
<stdarg.h>	functions with variable length argument lists
<stddef.h>	calculate the offset of fields within a structure
<stdio.h>	functions for input and output
<stdlib.h>	string conversion and memory allocation functions
<string.h>	functions to manipulate character arrays
<time.h>	functions to read and display time

3.3 Macro definitions

3.3.1 #define

Quite often, the same pattern of instructions will occur several times in a program. A macro instruction can be defined and used to generate these instructions every time the macro identifier is used in the source code.

The general form of a macro definition is

```
#define identifier text
```

The preprocessor will replace every occurrence of identifier with text. Notice that the text of a macro definition is never followed with a semicolon. It is a general rule that preprocessor statements are never terminated with a semicolon. Most macros are terminated with a semicolon when they are used in the body of a program but not when they are defined.

When macros are used they very often have the same appearance as function calls, but it is worth knowing the difference between macros and functions. Macros used in the source code of a program can look the same as function calls but the essential difference is that macros are expanded into source code whereas function calls are used to call sections of compiled code.

The preprocessor can be used to define, test and undefine macros. The program number defines a macro which substitutes an identifier, OLD_NUMBER, with a character string, "1234". This program also defines two macros called BEGIN and END which are used to replace the open and close braces.

```
/*
 * file name: number
 * demonstrate simple macro instructions
 */

#include <stdio.h>
#include <stdlib.h>

#define OLD_NUMBER 1234
#define BEGIN {
#define END }

int main(void)
  BEGIN
  int new_number;

  new_number = OLD_NUMBER;
  printf("New number = %d\n", new_number);
  exit(EXIT_SUCCESS);
  END
```

In this example the macro OLD_NUMBER, which is a symbolic constant and not a variable, is used by the preprocessor to replace every occurrence the string "OLD_NUMBER" in the source code with the string "1234". You must not think of macros as variables or anything else other than as a means of writing source code. When the macros BEGIN and END are typed in the source code the preprocessor replaces every occurrence of the macro BEGIN with the opening brace { and every occurrence of the macro END with the closing brace }. The program number is equivalent to the program processed. Notice that the symbolic constant

EXIT_SUCCESS, which is defined in the header file stdlib.h, is replaced with 0 in the program processed.

```
/*
 * file name: processed
 * a program equivalent to the program number
 */

#include <stdio.h>
#include <stdlib.h>

int main(void)
   {
   int new_number;

   new_number = 1234;
   printf("New number = %d\n", new_number);
   exit(0);
   }
```

3.3.2 Parameters

Macros can accept parameters and hand back values. The following code will define a macro which can be used to find the absolute value of any number passed to the macro as the parameter x.

```
#define absolute(x) ((x)<0 ? -(x) : (x))
```

This macro definition is read as "if x is less than zero then hand back the value -x else hand back x". When this macro is used in a program the parameter x can be any number so that, for example, absolute(-23) or absolute(1.23) can be used. We are not restricted to using the symbol x or any particular data type. The ? : version of the if-else construction used in the above definition is examined in more detail in chapter eight which deals with program control.

Macro instructions which accept parameters must be defined unambiguously. If the macro instruction absolute is defined as follows then the definition is ambiguous and can lead to incorrect results being handed back.

```
#define absolute(x) x<0 ? -x : x
```

This definition appears at first sight to be in order and can be read as "if x is less than zero then hand back -x else hand back x". A problem arises when x is a complex expression rather than a simple variable. Consider the macro expansion made by the preprocessor when x = a + b. The expanded code then becomes

```
a + b < 0 ? - a + b : a + b
```

which is read as "if a + b is less than zero then hand back -a + b else hand back a + b". This macro does not define the absolute value of a + b. In order to unambiguously hand back the absolute value of a + b the expanded code has to be

```
((a + b) < 0 ? -(a + b) : (a + b))
```

This unambiguous code is the expanded code for the macro defined as

```
#define absolute(x) ((x)<0 ? -(x) : (x))
```

Macro instructions which accept parameters are defined unambiguously only if each parameter is enclosed within parentheses and the whole text following the macro identifier is enclosed within parentheses. The correct and incorrect ways of defining macro instructions are demonstrated in the program correct.

```
/*
 * file name: correct
 * the correct and incorrect way to define macros
 */

#include <stdio.h>
#include <stdlib.h>

#define squright(x)  ((x)*(x))
#define squwrong(x)  x*x
#define absright(x)  ((x)<0 ? -(x) : (x))
#define abswrong(x)  x<0 ? -x : x

int main(void)
  {
  printf("(2+1) squared = %d\n", squright(2 + 1));
  printf("(2+1) squared != %d\n", squwrong(2 + 1));
  printf("absolute(-2+1) = %d\n", absright(-2 + 1));
  printf("absolute(-2+1) != %d\n", abswrong(-2 + 1));
  exit(EXIT_SUCCESS);
  }
```

When a macro such as absolute is used in the source code of a program then the expanded code is substituted where ever the macro absolute is used. This is not what happens if absolute is defined as a function. If absolute is defined as a function then the coding of the compiled function is called by the executing program and not substituted into the program before compilation.

You should never forget the differences between macros and functions. They can look the same but they are not the same. Macro instructions are substituted for their identifier in the source code of a program and, unlike functions, they can neither use recursion nor take function calls as parameters.

The definition of a macro instruction is sensitive to the use of white space characters. The incorrect macro definition

```
#define cubed (x) ((x)*(x)*(x))
```

will substitute the code "(x) ((x)*(x)*(x))" for the macro identifier "cubed" and not the code "((x)*(x)*(x))" for the identifier "cubed(x)". The correct definition for the above macro is

```
#define cubed(x) ((x)*(x)*(x))
```

The only difference between the incorrect and correct definitions is a white space character between cubed and (x). If the macro cubed is defined as a function instead of a macro then the white space character between cubed and (x) would not matter at all.

One of the most useful things about macro instructions is that a single macro can be used with different data types. This is not possible with equivalent functions which are sensitive to data types. This useful property of macro instructions is demonstrated in the program universal and this property can be a deciding factor when choosing between macro instructions and functions.

```
/*
 * file name: universal
 * macros can be used with most data types
 */

#include <stdio.h>
#include <stdlib.h>

#define squared(x) ((x)*(x))
#define cubed(x) ((x)*(x)*(x))

int main(void)
  {
  int cardinal = 2;
  double decimal = 3.0;
```

```
printf("2 squared = %d\n", squared(cardinal));
printf("3.0 cubed = %f\n", cubed(decimal));
exit(EXIT_SUCCESS);
}
```

3.3.3 #if, #else, #endif and #undef

A macro definition can only be made once in a program unless all the multiple definitions are identical. It might seem pointless to have more than one identical macro definition but it can be useful to have the same macro definition in a number of different header files. Doing this can save us the trouble of including a complete header file just to include one particular macro definition.

If we want to re-define a macro instruction then the directive #undef can be used to undefine the macro, releasing the macro identifier so that it can be re-defined with a new macro definition. If there is any doubt about whether or not a macro name has been used it is possible to use the #if #else #endif construction to test the macro name. For example

```
/*
 * file name: absolute
 * demonstrate the #if, #else, #endif and #undef direc-
     tives
 */

#include <stdio.h>
#include <stdlib.h>

#if defined(absolute)
  #undef absolute
  #define absolute(x) ((x) < 0 ? -(x) : (x))
#else
  #define absolute(x) ((x) < 0 ? -(x) : (x))
#endif

int main(void)
  {
  int result;

  result = absolute(-10 + 3);
  printf("absolute(-10 + 3) = %d\n", result);
  exit(EXIT_SUCCESS);
  }
```

The preprocessor conditional statement

```
#if !defined(identifier)
```

can be used in the same way as

```
#if defined(identifier)
```

but these two statements are the logical opposite of one another. The former is true if the identifier has not been defined and the latter is true if the identifier has been defined.

The directive #if can also be used in more general situations and #if is true if the expression following it is true. The #if directive is usually used in conditional compilations when, for example, you might want to print the values of certain variables in order to debug a program. An #if statement must be terminated with an #endif.

3.4 Debugging

In the program debug a symbolic constant DEBUG is assigned the value true and another BUGGED is assigned the value false in order to conditionally compile some rather artificial debugging statements. True and false are defined in some implementations of C, but it is always wise to use the preprocessor to check if they are defined in the version you are using. If they are not defined then, by convention, false is always defined as zero and true is defined as 1, although any non-zero number is recognized as true.

```
/*
 * file name: debug
 * demonstrate conditional compilation
 */

#include <stdio.h>
#include <stdlib.h>

#if !defined(TRUE)
  #define TRUE 1
  #define FALSE 0
#endif

#define DEBUG TRUE
#define BUGGED FALSE
```

```
#if !defined(absolute)
  #define absolute(x)  ((x) < 0 ? -(x) : (x))
#endif

int main(void)
  {
  int cardinal = -10;
  int result;

  result = absolute(cardinal);
  #if DEBUG
    printf("absolute(-10) = %d\n",result);
    /* compile only if debug = TRUE */
  #elif !BUGGED
    printf("absolute(1.23) = %f\n", absolute(1.23));
    /* compiled if DEBUG = FALSE and BUGGED = FALSE */
  #else
    #error force an error
  #endif
  exit(EXIT_SUCCESS);
  }
```

The #if (DEBUG) ... #elif ... #else ... #endif construction used in the program debug
cannot simply be replaced with /* ... */ to comment out the debugging code because
the commented out code would then contain comments, and nested comments are
illegal in C. The program debug uses the #elif directive which is a combination of
#else and #if. #elif is not paired with #endif but #if is always paired with #endif. For
example

```
#if DEBUG
  /* statements compiled only if DEBUG = TRUE */
#elif !BUGGED
  /* compiled if DEBUG = FALSE and BUGGED = FALSE */
#else
  #error force an error if DEBUG = FALSE and BUGGED = TRUE
#endif
```

The code above could be replaced with the following code

```
#if DEBUG
  /* statements compiled only if DEBUG = TRUE */
#else
  #if !BUGGED
    /* compiled if DEBUG = FALSE and BUGGED = FALSE */
```

```
  #else
     #error force an error if DEBUG = FALSE and BUGGED =
TRUE
   #endif
#endif
```

The second version requires that both #if statements are terminated with #endif and it
is logically equivalent to the first version.

3.5 #error

The #error directive can be used to conditionally abort a compilation even if your C
compiler does not implement the #error directive. The reason why this directive can
be used with a version of C which does not implement the #error directive is that
using #error generates a compiler error which halts the compilation and this is the
desired effect of the #error directive. The #error directive is implemented in ANSI C
and its use is demonstrated in the program error.

```
/*
 * file name: error
 * demonstrate the use of #error
 */

#include <stdio.h>
#include <stdlib.h>

#define absolute(x) DUMMY DEFINITION

#if !defined(absolute)
  #define absolute(x) ((x) < 0 ? -(x) : (x))
#else
  #error absolute already defined
#endif

int main(void)
   {
   int cardinal = -123;

   cardinal = absolute(cardinal);
   printf("absolute(-123) = %d\n", cardinal);
   exit(EXIT_SUCCESS);
   }
```

3.6 #line

The #line directive has the general form

```
#line line_number file_name
```

The #line directive is also used for debugging and causes the preprocessor to assign a new line number to the line following the #line directive. For example, the command

```
#line 100
```

assigns the line number 100 to the next line of the source code. The optional file_name identifier is used to assign a new file name to the current file.

The #line directive does not seem to be very useful. The program line demonstrates the use of #line and this program forces a compiler error in line 102. If you edit the program and delete the #line statement then the error will be generated in line 10.

```
/*
 * file name: line
 * demonstrate the use of #line
 */

int main(void)
  {
  #line 100
  /* this will be line 100 */

  #error error in line 102
  exit(EXIT_SUCCESS);
  }
```

3.7 The string generating character

If a parameter in a macro definition is preceded by the string generating character, #, then that parameter is enclosed in double quotes in the macro expansion. The macro format is defined in the program strgen as follows

```
#define format(x,c) printf(#x" = %"#c"\n",x)
```

When the macro format is typed in the source code with, for example

```
format(number,d);
```

it expands to

```
printf("number"" = %""d""\n",d);
```

which is equivalent to

```
printf("number = %d\n", d);
```

This macro can be used to print the variable identifier and the value of any type of variable. This would not be possible with a function call.

```
/*
 * file name: strgen
 * using the string generating character
 */

#include <stdio.h>
#include <stdlib.h>

#define format(x,c) printf(#x" = %"#c"\n",x)

int main(void)
  {
  char letter = 'C';
  int cardinal = 2;
  double decimal = 3.0;

  format(letter,c);
  format(cardinal,d);
  format(decimal,f);
  exit(EXIT_SUCCESS);
  }
```

3.8 The concatenation operator

The concatenation operator can be used to join together, or concatenate, character strings to make new identifiers. This is quite unusual and demonstrated in the program concat where the components of two identifiers, var_one and var_two, are concatenated by the macro concat. The identifiers are concatenated from the component var (in the macro definition) and from the arguments _one and _two.

```
/*
 * file name: concat
 * using the concatenation operator ##
 */

#include <stdio.h>
#include <stdlib.h>

#define concat(a,b,c)  a[b] = var##c

int main(void)
  {
  int list[5];
  int table[5];
  int var_one = 11;
  int var_two = 22;

  concat(list, 3, _one); /* list[3] = var_one; */
  concat(table, 4, _two); /* table[4] = var_two; */
  printf("list[3] = %d\n", list[3]);
  printf("table[4] = %d\n", table[4]);
  exit(EXIT_SUCCESS);
  }
```

3.9 #pragma

Pragma statements are used for tasks such as marking the beginning and the end of a piece of assembly language, and so on. Pragmas are system dependent preprocessor commands and although they are allowed in ANSI C source code they inevitably lead to non-portable source code, even from one ANSI compiler to another on the same hardware. For this reason pragmas will not be used in this book.

Declaring data types

4.1 Declaring variables

BASIC programmers will be familiar with the idea of identifying a variable type by its name, or more formally, its identifier. BASIC integer variables use the suffix %, string variables use the suffix $, and floating point variables use only alpha-numeric characters in their identifiers. These conventions do not exist in C and all variables have to be declared as being of a particular type before they can be used. Declaring a variable means associating the variable identifier with a variable type.

Declaring a variable defines how much space will be made available to store the data associated with the variable, it limits the type and range of values the variable can store, and names the storage location of the variable. The variable type will also determine the speed with which data can be handled in computations. Most implementations of C are optimised to run as fast as possible with data stored in variables of type int and generally 32 bit integers will be processed quicker than 16 bit integers.

As you become more experienced in C you will find that there are a number of advantages to be gained from having to declare variables rather than adopting the BASIC haphazard use of variables. The main advantage seems to be that declaring variables forces the programmer to think carefully about program design and encourages a more structured and ordered approach to programming. An incidental advantage is that declaring variables helps to find any misspelt identifiers because misspelt identifiers generate errors during compilation.

There are four basic data types used in C. These basic types are characters, integers, floating point numbers and pointers.

Characters are the letters of the alphabet, the numbers 0 to 9 and a number of special symbols including * / % & and so on. Characters are stored using either the ASCII or EBCDIC 8 bit codes.

An integer is any positive or negative whole number without a decimal point. The range of numbers that can be stored as integers depends on the number of bytes allocated to the integer. If two bytes are available then the range for integers is from -32768 to +32767 but if four bytes are allocated to each integer then the range is from -2147483648 to +2147483647.

Floating point numbers are positive or negative numbers with a decimal point. Floating point numbers are sometimes referred to as single precision numbers. Double precision numbers are also floating point numbers but with a more precise representation of the number than that used for single precision numbers. The range of values available to single precision numbers is much less than the range of values available to double precision numbers and, as their data types suggest, double precision numbers have at least twice the precision of floating point numbers.

A pointer is a special type of integer variable which is used to store the address of another variable. A pointer to a floating point variable stores the integer address of the first byte of that variable. Pointers store addresses as integers but pointers and integers are not directly interchangable. Characters, integers and floating point numbers are dealt with in this chapter and pointers have a chapter to themselves in chapter ten.

Some of the basic data types have a number of variations and there are ten reserved words used to declare variable types in the ANSI standard for C compilers. There is some redundancy in the naming of the types because, for example, short is the same type as short int and long double is the same as double. In the ANSI standard all the variable types can be prefixed with the qualifier unsigned if only positive numbers are to be used. The ANSI standard also includes the qualifier signed, meaning both positive and negative numbers, which is the default for all data types except char.

It is possible to define new data types if the ones provided are not suitable for your application. We can, for example, define a variable type to cope with imaginary numbers. Defining new data types is dealt with in chapter 13.

The following data types and data type qualifiers are provided by all ANSI C compilers and they are all reserved words.

char

A single character. The values assigned to variables of type char are single characters. The ASCII character set is represented by characters with integer values from 0 to 127. Single characters are enclosed in single quotes, for example, 'A', 'a' and so on. Strings of characters are enclosed in double quotes, for example "this is a string".

Because C compilers are most efficient using type int you should only use type char for single characters or to define arrays for storing character strings. Do not use type char for small integers. Data items of type char are unsigned by default but they can be explicitly declared as signed char or unsigned char.

short

A 16 bit integer. The data types short and short int are equivalent and both define a 16 bit integer. A signed short integer can be assigned a value in the range from -32768 to 32767. The signed integers from -32768 to -1 are represented by the hexadecimal numbers 8000 to FFFF and the signed integers from 0 to 32767 are represented by the hexadecimal numbers from 0 to 7FFF. For this reason the signed integers from -32768 to 32767 are represented by the hexadecimal numbers from 8000 to 7FFF. An unsigned short integer can be assigned a value in the range 0 to 65535 (hex 0 to hex FFFF).

short int

A 16 bit integer, the same as short.

int

A 32 bit integer. The data types int, long, and long int are all equivalent and specify a long, or 32 bit, integer. A signed 32 bit integer can be assigned a value in the range from -2147483648 to 2147483647 (hex 80000000 to hex 7FFFFFFF) and an unsigned 32 bit integer can be assigned a value in the range from 0 to 4294967295 (hex 0 to hex FFFFFFFF).

long

A 32 bit integer, the same as int.

long int

A 32 bit integer, the same as long.

float

A floating point number. By convention, floating point variables should not be used to pass arguments to mathematical functions, only type double or long double should be used. Floating point numbers have a range from $\pm$ 1.17 e-38 to $\pm$ 3.40 e+38 with six decimal digits of precision. (Acorn ANSI C).

double

A double precision floating point number. Only double precision floating point numbers should be used to pass arguments to mathematical functions. Range $\pm$ 2.22 e-308 to $\pm$ 1.79 e+308 with 15 decimal digits of precision. (Acorn ANSI C).

long double

A double precision floating point number, the same as double.

enum

Enumerated data type. A user-defined data type made up of a set of words instead of numbers or characters. The words are mapped onto integer constants by the compiler and these constants are used to identify the enum data type. This allows the programmer to use meaningful identifiers in situations where less meaningful numbers or characters would normally be used.

void

C makes extensive use of functions and in the bad old days before ANSI C functions which were not declared as returning values of a specific type could return a value which was either an integer type or nothing at all. In ANSI C the default data type for a function is integer and so all functions which are not declared as a specific data type can only return integer values. Functions which return no value at all now have to be qualified as data type void.

It is possible to qualify variables as type void but there is no point in declaring variables other than pointers as type void. A void pointer can be used as a pointer to any data type and this is quite useful.

volatile

Variables qualified as data type volatile can have their value altered by processes outside the control of the program. These can include the registers used for memory mapped input and output, for real time clocks and so on.

const

Constants can be qualified as data type const. Constants must be assigned a value when they are declared and that value cannot be changed during program execution.

4.2 The size of variables

Declaring and initialising local variables is demonstrated in the program sizes which will display the number of bytes used by six data types. Compile, link and execute this program. It is quite interesting to compare the number of bytes used by different variable types with each other.

```
/*
 * file name: sizes
 * print variable and string sizes
 */

#include <stdio.h>
#include <string.h>
#include <stdlib.h>

int main(void)
  {
  char a;
  short b;
  int c;
  const int d;
  long e;
  float f;
  double g;
  static char text[] = "0123456789";

  printf("The size of char is %d byte\n", sizeof(a));
  printf("The size of short is %d bytes\n", sizeof(b));
  printf("The size of int is %d bytes\n", sizeof(c));
  printf("The size of const int is %d bytes\n",
      sizeof(d));
  printf("The size of long is %d bytes\n", sizeof(e));
  printf("The size of float is %d bytes\n", sizeof(f));
  printf("The size of double is %d bytes\n", sizeof(g));
  printf("10 bytes of text are stored in %d bytes\n",
      strlen(text)+1);
  printf("including a zero end-of-string marker.");
  exit(EXIT_SUCCESS);
  }
```

The program sizes also displays the amount of storage required for character strings stored in char arrays. Character strings are examined in much more detail in chapter 12.

To declare a variable it is necessary to write the variable type followed by a list of the variable identifiers of that type. For example, to declare two long integers called cardinal and ordinal use the following code

```
long int cardinal, ordinal;
```

This declaration is equivalent to the following, and either could be used

```
long cardinal, ordinal;
```

A variable identifier can be up to 31 characters long and must start with either an alphabetic character or the underscore. In ANSI C all 31 characters of an identifier are significant. Any alpha-numeric character or the underscore can be used in the identifier but you must not use a function identifier or a reserved word as a variable identifier. It is the usual practice to reserve variable identifiers starting with the underscore for system use. For this reason we should avoid using the underscore as the first character in any of our own identifiers.

4.3 Scope of variables

Variables can be either global or local. Global variables are available to all the functions in a program but local variables are only available to the function within which they are declared. It is considered to be good practice to only use global variables when it is impractical to use local ones.

4.3.1 Global variables

Global variables are usually declared in the global white space after the preprocessor commands and before the definition of the function main, but they can be declared anywhere outside the functions. Global variables are available to all the functions and modules of a program. If a global variable is to be used in a function then you should use the keyword extern to make the variable available to the function. This is demonstrated in the program global which initialises the global variable in the function funct. This has only been done as an illustration, it could have been initialised in main.

The program global also demonstrates the use of function prototypes. The function main calls the user-defined function funct. The first line of the definition of funct is

```
void funct(void)
```

This defines the function as a void function, i.e. one that does not return a value, and the function does not accept any parameters. The function prototype is a copy of this first line of the definition terminated with a semicolon, placed immediately after the opening brace of the main function. Function prototypes in the calling function make the called function available and allow some error checking to take place.

```
/*
 * file name: global
 * declare and initialise a global variable
 */

#include <stdio.h>
#include <stdlib.h>

int cardinal;

int main(void)
  {
  void funct(void);
  extern int cardinal;

  funct();
  printf("cardinal = %d\n", cardinal);
  exit(EXIT_SUCCESS);
  }

void funct(void)
  {
  extern int cardinal;

  cardinal = 123;
  return;
  }
```

4.3.2 Local variables

Local variables are declared immediately after any function prototypes which follow the opening brace of a function. For example

```
/*
 * file name: local
 * declare local variables
 */
```

```
#include <stdio.h>
#include <stdlib.h>

int main(void)
  {
  void funct(void);
  int cardinal;

  cardinal = 1234;
  printf("cardinal = %d\n", cardinal);
  funct();
  exit(EXIT_SUCCESS);
  }

void funct(void)
  {
  double decimal;

  decimal = 1.234;
  printf("decimal = %f\n", decimal);
  return;
  }
```

4.4 Initialising variables

In the two examples immediately above, the global and local variables are first declared and then initialised. The variables are made available by declaring them but their values are unknown and unpredictable until they are initialised. There are two equivalent ways of initialising variables and both involve declaring a variable and then assigning a value to the variable. These two methods are illustrated below.

```
int cardinal;
cardinal = 123;
```

This is equivalent to

```
int cardinal = 123;
```

Both methods can be used with all numeric data types and either method will result in the same size application code. Which method you chose to use will depend on factors such as the legibility of the source code but not on the size of the application code.

4.5 The cast operator

A variable of type float can be declared and assigned a value with the following statement

```
float decimal = (float) 6.0;
```

This might seem a little strange at first but the reason for it is that the floating point number 6.0 is, by default, a double precision number but a variable of type float is a single precision variable. This is an example of casting and the double precision number 6.0 is said to be cast into a single precision number and then assigned to the variable decimal.

The cast operator can be used to convert one data type into another. The following code can be used to convert the number stored in a floating point variable called decimal into an integer which can then be assigned to an integer variable called cardinal.

```
cardinal = (int) decimal;
```

The integer variable will be assigned the value of the truncated floating point variable so that if the variable decimal stores the value 12.34 then the variable cardinal is assigned the value 12. The reverse operation could be performed with the following code in which the variable decimal is assigned the floating point representation of the integer variable cardinal.

```
decimal = (float) cardinal;
```

Cast operations can be performed using any data type but it does not always make sense to do so. Some simple cast operations are demonstrated in the program cast.

```
/*
 * file name: cast
 * demonstrate the cast operator
 */

#include <stdio.h>
#include <stdlib.h>

int main(void)
  {
  char letter;
  int cardinal;
  double decimal;
```

```
letter = 'A';
cardinal = (int) letter;
decimal = (double) letter;
printf ("letter = %c\n", letter);
printf ("(int) letter = %d\n", cardinal);
printf ("(double) letter = %f\n\n", decimal);
cardinal = 65;
letter = (char) cardinal;
decimal = (double) cardinal;
printf ("cardinal = %d\n", cardinal);
printf ("(char) cardinal = %c\n", letter);
printf ("(double) cardinal = %f\n\n", decimal);
decimal = 65.4321;
letter = (char) decimal;
cardinal = (int) decimal;
printf ("decimal = %f\n", decimal);
printf ("(char) decimal = %c\n", letter);
printf ("(int) decimal = %d\n", cardinal);
exit(EXIT_SUCCESS);
}
```

4.6 Enumerated data types

Enumerated data types are defined using the reserved word enum followed by the type identifier and then a list of acceptable values for the data type in braces. For example

```
enum PIGMENT {red, green, blue};
```

A variable declared as type PIGMENT can subsequently only take one of the values red, green or blue. Red will be represented by the integer 0, green will be represented by integer 1, and blue will be represented by integer 2. A variable can be declared as type PIGMENT and initialised after the enumerated data type has been defined.

```
int main(void)
  {
  enum PIGMENT {red, green, blue};
  enum PIGMENT ink = red;

  /* statements */
  }
```

In the outline program above the variable ink is declared as a variable of the enumerated data type PIGMENT and it is initialised with the value red. The value red is represented by, but not the same as, integer 0. The enumerated data type is useful because the value red is a meaningful identifier instead of the less meaningful equivalent integer zero. Variables declared as enumerated types can be assigned values such as red, green or blue, and compared to variables or values of their type.

The range of acceptable values in the above example is deliberately and usefully restricted to the values red, green or blue. You cannot assign a value that has not been enumerated when the variable is defined. Enumerated data types can be global or local, depending on where the are defined, and you can use the cast operator to cast user-defined enumerated data types into integers, or vice versa.

```
/*
 * file name: pigments
 * demonstrate enum data type
 */

#include <stdio.h>
#include <stdlib.h>

int main(void)
  {
  enum PIGMENT {red, green, blue};
  enum PIGMENT ink = blue;
  int cardinal = 1;

  printf("Blue is equivalent to integer %d\n", (int) ink);
  ink = (enum PIGMENT) cardinal;
  if (ink == green)
  printf("%d is equivalent to pigment green\n", cardinal);
  ink = red;
  printf("Red is equivalent to integer %d\n", (int) ink);
  exit(EXIT_SUCCESS);
  }
```

4.7 Constants

The variables used in a program are always given identifiers. Constants are different to variables in that they may or may not have identifiers and their values never change. Consider a simple equation for calculating speed in miles per hour from the speed in knots.

```
mph = knots * 1.151515
```

In this equation mph and knots are variables and 1.151515, a conversion factor, is a constant. The conversion factor can be assigned to a constant using the reserved word const.

```
/*
 * file name: knots
 * demonstrate the use of const
 */

#include <stdio.h>
#include <stdlib.h>

int main(void)
  {
  double knots = 20;
  double mph;
  const double factor = 1.151515;
  mph = knots * factor;
  printf("knots = %f\n", knots);
  printf("mph = %f\n", mph);
  exit(EXIT_SUCCESS);
  }
```

4.8 Symbolic data types

The keyword typedef is used to create symbolic data types. If you are not happy with the identifiers given to data types by C then you can change the identifiers of existing data types (and define new data types) with the compiler directive typedef. We can, for example, define a symbolic data type called BYTE with the following code

```
typedef char BYTE;
```

and then use the symbolic data type BYTE to declare variables which would normally have been defined as type char, for example

```
typedef char BYTE;
BYTE letter, symbol;
```

This declaration is equivalent to

```
char letter, symbol;
```

The typedef statement is used in the same way as a declaration. It is written inside a function for local definitions or outside the functions for global definitions. The keyword typedef can be used to reduce the amount of typing when complex declarations are used. Symbolic data types are written in capital letters to distinguish them from other data types.

We can define a new variable type with typedef but we cannot define a storage class using this keyword. Storage classes will be dealt with in the next chapter.

5

Variable storage classes

5.1 The attributes of variables

Every variable has three attributes – type, value and storage class. The type attribute is established in a declaration statement, and a variable can be type char, int, double and so on. A variable can be assigned a value either when it is declared or later in the body of the program. There are four storage classes – automatic, external, static, and register and every variable has a storage class, even if the storage class is not declared explicitly.

The storage class associated with a variable is established at the same time as the variable type, that is, when the variable is declared. If the class is not declared explicitly then the variable takes a default class which is automatic for local variables and static for global variables.

5.2 Automatic variables

The keyword auto is used to declare the automatic storage class. An automatic variable is one which is only available to the statements in the function within which the automatic variable is declared. The scope of an automatic variable is said to be local to the function within which it is declared.

If an automatic variable is declared in two separate functions and the same identifier is used for both variables then the compiler recognizes the two identically named automatic variables as different and distinct from one another.

All local variables, including automatic variables, are declared after the function prototypes which follow the opening brace of a function. Automatic variables become active when a function is called and cease to exist when the function returns control to its calling function. An active automatic variable is not normally available to any other function called while the variable is active because an automatic variable is always a local variable.

The value stored in an automatic variable can be passed to another function as an argument and values can be returned to an automatic variable from other functions, but the variable itself is not normally made directly available to those other functions. An exception can be made to this rule because a pointer can be used to make an automatic variable directly accessible to functions other than the one within which it is declared. The techniques involved in using pointers are described in chapter ten.

Automatic variables are kept on a stack on top of the return address used by the function in which they are declared. The automatic variables are popped off the stack and lost when a return is made from the function. In this way they only use memory when the function in which they are declared is active and using automatic variables rather than external or static variables can reduce the amount of memory used by a program.

The keyword auto, used to declare automatic variables, is optional because all local variables are automatic by default. The explicit declaration of automatic variables with the keyword auto is demonstrated in the program auto.

```c
/*
 * file name: auto
 * declare an automatic variable
 */

#include <stdio.h>
#include <stdlib.h>

int main(void)
  {
  void funct(void);
  auto int cardinal = 123;

  printf("cardinal = %d\n",cardinal);
  funct();
  exit(EXIT_SUCCESS);
  }

void funct(void)
  {
  auto double decimal = 1.2345;
```

```
printf("decimal = %f\n", decimal);
return;
}
```

5.3 External variables

An external variable is the C equivalent of a global variable, and the terms external and global tend to be used interchangeably. An external variable is available to all the modules and functions of a program and it has to be declared once outside the functions, usually in the global white space between the #include statements and the first line of the definition of the function main, and again in every function which uses the variable. The keyword extern is not used when an external variable is first declared outside the functions but it is used to declare the variable in each function which uses the variable. The keyword extern is used in a function to refer to a previously declared external variable.

The program external, which demonstrates the declaration of an external variable and the subsequent use of the keyword extern, has been split into two distinct modules. These modules should be stored in two separate files and compiled separately. The two object files can then be linked with the standard ANSI library to make an application file.

The program external is a simple and somewhat artificial example of splitting a program into distinct modules but the principle of splitting programs in this way is a good one because it allows a programmer to develop and debug a program one module at a time. All programs with more than one function should be developed in modules and then there is no need to re-compile the whole program every time a module is edited. Only the edited module needs to be re-compiled and then all the object files can be linked to make the application file. The mechanics of separate compilation and linking are very straightforward but they tend to vary in detail from one implementation to another. You should refer to your C manual for more information.

The use of the keyword extern to declare an external variable within a function is optional in any function in the same module as the initial global declaration of the external variable. In the example program external the use of the keyword extern is optional in main because main is in the same module as the global declaration of the external variable. The statement

```
extern int cardinal;
```

in main can be replaced with

```
int cardinal;
```

But the same substitution cannot be made in the function funct. The use of the keyword extern is mandatory in funct because the initial global declaration of the variable cardinal is in a different module.

```
/*
 * file name: external
 * declare and initialise an external variable
 */

#include <stdio.h>
#include <stdlib.h>

int cardinal;

int main(void)
  {
  void funct(void);
  extern int cardinal;

  funct();
  printf("cardinal = %d, printed in main\n", cardinal);
  exit(EXIT_SUCCESS);
  }

/*
 * file name: extmodb
 * use a separate file for this module
 */

#include <stdio.h>

void funct(void)
  {
  extern int cardinal;

  cardinal = 123;
  printf("cardinal assigned %d in function\n", cardinal);
  return;
  }
```

Although the use of the keyword extern is optional when the initial global declaration is in the same module as the functions which use the variable, it is a good idea to always use the keyword extern to declare an external variable in any function. Using extern in all functions will remind the programmer that he or she is using an external variable.

External variables must be used with care. They tend to eat up memory and, more importantly, they can make programs unstructured and difficult to debug. Functions which use external variables are not usually portable to other programs and for these reasons external or global variables are often used only as a last resort or when using local variables makes a program untidy or difficult to follow.

If at all possible you should avoid using external variables in a program. You may be tempted to use them because they appear to simplify a program – but this is an illusion. A program which uses external variables may require less coding but the application file will often be more unwieldy than a program which uses local variables. Local variables can always be passed to other functions as arguments and values can be returned to local variables from functions. Using local rather than global variables will simplify debugging, make functions portable to other programs and give you keyboard credibility with other programmers.

5.4 Static variables

Static variables can be either local or global variables, and all global variables are static variables by default. The essential difference between an automatic and a static variable is the value of a static variable does not disappear when the function of which it is a part returns control to its calling function. The values stored in static variables have the permanence that automatic variables lack.

The scope of a static local variable is the same as that of an automatic local variable but because the value of a static variable is kept intact when the return statement is executed that value will still be available the next time the function is called. The memory allocated to a static variable is available as long as the program of which it is a part is still running.

The following example shows how local static variables are declared with the keyword static. The first time the function funct is called the variables cardinal and decimal already have the values 1 and 4.0 respectively. These values are assigned to the static variables during compilation. They are not assigned when the function is called. During the first call to funct the value assigned to the variable cardinal is incremented (cardinal++) and value stored in the variable decimal is squared (decimal *= decimal). These values are retained after control is returned to main. When funct is called a second time the variables cardinal and decimal still have the values 2 and 16.0 that were assigned to them during the first function call.

```
/*
 * file name: static
 * static local variables
 */

#include <stdio.h>
#include <stdlib.h>

int main(void)
  {
  void funct(void);

  funct();
  funct();
  exit(EXIT_SUCCESS);
  }

void funct(void)
  {
  static int cardinal = 1;
  static double decimal = 4.0;
  printf("cardinal = %d\n", cardinal);
  printf("decimal = %f\n", decimal);
  cardinal++;
  decimal *= decimal;
  return;
  }
```

5.5 Register variables

A computer CPU chip has internal registers that can be used for many things including the storage of variables. If registers are available for storing variables then using them will speed up the execution of a program.

Registers can be used to store variables of type char and int as well as pointers to any type of variable. Registers cannot be used to store any type of floating point number. If an appropriate register is not available then a variable with a register storage class will revert to an automatic variable of the appropriate type.

Register variables can be declared by using the keyword register followed by the data type and variable identifier. The program register uses the register storage class for the integer variable loop. Declaring the variable loop as a register variable will speed up the execution of the for loop when compared with declaring an equivalent automatic variable.

```
/*
 * file name: register
 * declare register variable
 */

#include <stdio.h>
#include <stdlib.h>

int main(void)
  {
  register int loop;

  for (loop = 0; loop < 10; loop++)
    {
    printf("loop = %d\n", loop);
    }
  exit(EXIT_SUCCESS);
  }
```

Although six registers are available in Acorn ANSI C it is advisable to declare no more than four register variables. If more than four are declared then this storage class may be treated as automatic and the variables will then be held in memory rather than in registers. Your C manual will tell you how many register variables are available with other implementations.

Input and Output

6.1 The standard input and output files

Almost every C program which performs any useful purpose will have some provision for reading the keyboard and writing to the VDU screen. The keyboard is known formally as the standard input file, stdin, and the VDU is known formally as the standard output file, stdout.

The standard input and output header file, stdio.h, provides quite a number of functions to be used for input and output. There are three pairs of basic I/O functions defined in stdio.h and most of the other functions are variations on these basic functions. The basic functions are printf and scanf, puts and gets, and putchar and getchar.

The function printf is used to write to the standard output file, stdout, i.e. the VDU screen. The function scanf is used to read the standard input file, stdin, i.e. the keyboard. The functions puts, gets, putchar and getchar are used for string output, string input, character output, and character input respectively.

In order to use any of the i/o functions it is always necessary to include the stdio.h file with the preprocessor command

```
#include <stdio.h>
```

6.2 The function printf

The formatted output function printf is provided with every implementation of C and has the general form

```
n = printf(control_string, item_1, item_2, ... item_n);
```

The control string is mandatory and as its name suggests it determines or controls the format for writing variables or character strings identified as item_1, item_2 and so on. The control string can be followed by any number of data items, including no data items.

The function printf returns an integer value equal to the number of characters printed. If there is an error printf returns a negative value. It is common practice to ignore the value returned by printf and to use it as if it's a void function.

The program simple is an example of using printf to print a message on the VDU. This program does not use any data items and the control string is simply a text message which starts and ends with a new line character, represented by the escape sequence \n.

```
/*
 * file name: simple
 * simple demonstration of printf
 */

#include <stdio.h>
#include <stdlib.h>

int main(void)
  {
  printf("\nHello World\n");
  exit(EXIT_SUCCESS);
  }
```

The control string can contain conversion specifiers as well as text and escape sequences.

6.2.1 printf conversion specifiers

Conversion specifiers are typed within the control string and are used to determine the way in which the optional data items are printed. There must be a conversion specifier for every optional data item although the control string can contain the special conversion specifier %% which is not associated with a data item.

A conversion specifier starts with a percent sign which is followed by a character code to determine the output format of the associated data item. In the program bodyheat the conversion specifier %f is used to print a double precision floating point number.

```
/*
 * file name: bodyheat
 * print a floating point variable
 */

#include <stdio.h>
#include <stdlib.h>

int main(void)
  {
  double temperature = 98.4;

  printf("Temperature = %f\n", temperature);
  exit(EXIT_SUCCESS);
  }
```

The variable temperature in the program bodyheat is a double precision floating point variable which is assigned the value 98.4. If you compile, link and execute this program then the function printf will produce the following output

```
Temperature = 98.400000
```

The conversion specifier in the control string will be replaced with the value assigned to the variable temperature.

The following printf conversion specifiers are available in ANSI C.

Identifier	Format
%d	decimal integer
%i	decimal integer
%c	single character
%s	character string
%f	floating point or double, decimal notation
%e or %E	floating point or double, exponential notation
%g or %G	%e, %E or %f, whichever is shorter
%u	decimal integer converted to unsigned integer
%o	octal integer, without leading zero
%x or %X	hexadecimal integer, without leading 0x or 0X
%p	pointer, hexadecimal address
%n	number of characters printed so far
%%	print the % character

The output produced by all the conversion specifiers is right justified but this can be modified by extending the specifiers.

To produce left justified output a minus sign, usually called a minus flag, is placed after the percent sign. The optional minus flag can be followed by other optional flags, an optional format specifier, an optional modifier and a mandatory specifier character.

6.2.2 The general form of printf conversion specifiers

The printf conversion specifier has the following general form in which square brackets are used to indicate optional parts of the conversion specifier.

```
% [flags] [field_width] [.precision] [modifier] character
```

The optional flags are – + 0 and #. The minus flag is used to specify left justification. If it is not included then right justification is used. The plus flag is used if a number is to be printed with a + prefix if it is positive and a – prefix if it is negative. Without the + flag only negative numbers are prefixed with a sign. The zero flag is used to pad numbers with zeros on the left. The # flag is used to prefix octal and hexadecimal numbers with 0 and 0x respectively and to ensure that floating point numbers are always printed with a decimal point. The flags can be typed in any order.

The optional field width specifier is a number used to determine the minimum number of characters to be used to display the value assigned to the associated data item. If the data item uses less than this minimum number then the unused characters are padded out with spaces, or zeros if the zero flag is used. If the data item requires more characters than the minimum specified in the field width then more characters are made available.

The optional precision, always preceded with a period, follows the field width and has different interpretations depending on the data item type. For floating point variables it specifies the number of digits after the decimal point. For string output it specifies how many characters are to be printed. For integers it specifies the minimum number of digits to be printed, with leading zeros if necessary.

The optional modifier can be either h, l or L. The modifier h is used if the argument is short or unsigned short, l (lower case L) is used for long or unsigned long and L is used for long double.

The specifier character is mandatory and represents any one of the conversion characters d, c, s, f and so on.

The following examples are all legal conversion specifiers

%f	floating point, right justified
%-u	unsigned integer, left justified

%-#10.2f	floating point, left justified, 10 character field width, 2 characters after the decimal point
%-20.19s	string, left justified, 20 character field width, 19 characters printed

The use of a more complex conversion specifier is illustrated in the program icecold. This program also displays the number of characters printed in the first call to printf.

```
/*
 * file name: icecold
 * print a floating point variable
 */

#include <stdio.h>
#include <stdlib.h>

int main(void)
  {
  double temperature = 32.0;
  int number;

  printf("Temperature = %-4.1f%n\n", temperature,
      &number);
  printf("number = %d\n", number);
  exit(EXIT_SUCCESS);
  }
```

In this case the variable temperature will be printed left justified, the field width of the data printed from the variable will be 4 characters and there will be one character to the right of the decimal point. The following output will be produced displaying the value of the variable temperature and the number of characters printed by the first call to printf.

```
 Temperature = 32.0
 number = 18
```

The optional field width and precision specifiers can be replaced with an asterisk. If you substitute either or both of these specifiers with an asterisk then the data item to which the specifier applies must be preceded by one or two integer arguments which specify the field width and/or precision respectively. This technique is used to produce variable conversion specifiers and is demonstrated in the program asterisk.

```
/*
 * file name: asterisk
 * variable field width and precision
 */

#include <stdio.h>
#include <stdlib.h>

int main(void)
  {
  int width = 4;
  int precision = 1;
  double temperature = 98.4;

  printf("temperature = %*.*f\n",
         width, precision, temperature);
  exit(EXIT_SUCCESS);
  }
```

6.2.3 Printing long integers

Printing long integer values using printf requires the use of a lower case l to be used as a modifier in the control sequence. To display a long integer use the control sequence %ld or %li as shown in the program longint. This program also uses the special conversion specifier %% to print the percent symbol. The specifier %% is not associated with a data item.

```
/*
 * file name: longint
 * demonstrate the use of conversion modifiers
 */

#include <stdio.h>
#include <stdlib.h>

int main(void)
  {
  long int big = 123456L;

  printf("Incorrect specifier %%d, 123456L = %d\n", big);
  /* the above statement will generate a warning */
  printf("Correct specifier %%ld, 123456L = %ld\n", big);
  /* this statement shows how it should be done */
```

```
exit(EXIT_SUCCESS);
}
```

Unsigned integers are used to store positive integers only. Standard integers can store the values -2147483648 to 2147483647 (hex 80000000 to hex 7FFFFFFF) and unsigned integers can store the values 0 to 4294967295 (hex 0 to hex FFFFFFFF). Unsigned integers are declared and initialised with, for example

```
unsigned int cardinal = 60000;
```

Displaying unsigned integers with printf requires the use of the conversion specifier %u instead of the specifiers %d or %i which should only be used for signed integers.

6.2.4 printf escape sequences

Optional escape sequences can be used in the printf control string and they are sometimes referred to as backslash codes. The backslash character is used in the control string to provide an escape from the normal interpretation of the character following the backslash. The backslash character alters the meaning of the next character in the control string.

Escape sequences are used for control purposes and can be used to send special codes to the standard output file. There are several special escape sequences used to send specific characters as well as two general purpose escape sequences which can send any ASCII character. The special escape sequences are

Escape sequence	*Meaning*
\a	send the bell character to the output file
\b	send the backspace character
\f	send form feed
\n	line feed
\r	carriage return
\t	horizontal tab
\v	vertical tab
\\	send the backslash character
\'	send single quote
\"	double quote
\0	null character (ASCII 0)

The escape sequences do not necessarily correspond with their equivalent control codes. The control code for bell is CTRL+G but the escape sequence is \a, the control code for carriage return is CTRL+M but the escape sequence is \r, and so on.

There are two general purpose escape sequences used to send either an octal or a hexadecimal number to represent any ASCII character.

Escape sequence	*Meaning*
\xhh	send the hexadecimal character represented by hh
\ooo	send the octal character represented by ooo

The hexadecimal numbers can be in the range from 00 to 7F and you must include a leading zero for numbers 00 to 0F so that there are always three characters in the backslash code. Octal numbers can be in the range from 000 to 177 and again you must include leading zeros if necessary to make up three characters in the backslash code. The reason for restricting the use of hexadecimal and octal numbers to values in the range from 00 to 7F is that values greater than hex 7F or octal 177 will have the sign bit set and the interpretation of these numbers will be implementation dependent.

The program octal demonstrates how the octal and hexadecimal escape sequences can be used and also how to write printable quotation marks in the printf control string with \".

```
/*
 * file name: octal
 * printing octal and hexadecimal backslash codes
 */

#include <stdio.h>
#include <stdlib.h>

int main(void)
  {
  printf("My name in octal is ");
  printf("\"\107\157\162\144\157\156\"\n"); /* "Gordon"\n */
  printf("and in hexadecimal ");
  printf("\"\x47\x6f\x72\x64\x6f\x6e\"\n"); /* "Gordon"\n */
  exit(EXIT_SUCCESS);
  }
```

6.3 The function scanf

The function scanf complements the function printf. The function scanf is a formatted input function which can be used to read the standard input file which is, by default, the keyboard.

A number of the following programs will demonstrate using scanf to read the keyboard and, if you use the demonstration programs, you will soon find that scanf is usually quite unsuitable for use with the keyboard. The main reason why scanf is unsuitable is that C treats the keyboard as an input file and expects the information taken from the keyboard to match an input format as if the data is taken from a machine formatted file. Computer users typing at a keyboard are usually much less reliable than machine formatted files and often fail to adopt the exact format required by scanf.

Even if you never use scanf in programs which involve keyboard interaction it is still important to know how scanf is used because a related function called fscanf is used to read disk files. A knowledge of scanf will allow you to convert programs which use scanf to a more suitable input function. The functions gets, fgets and getchar are almost always the preferred functions for keyboard input.

The function scanf appears at first sight to be quite similar to its complementary function printf but there are some important differences between the two functions. The scanf function has the following general form

```
n = scanf(control_string, pointer_1, pointer_2, ...
    pointer_n);
```

A very important difference between printf and scanf is that printf uses variable identifiers in its list of data items but scanf uses pointers to variables.

6.3.1 scanf control string

The control string is mandatory and as its name suggests it determines or controls the format for reading the data items which are pointed to by pointer_1, pointer_2, and so on. Unlike the printf control string, the scanf control string cannot contain a message but usually only consists of conversion specifiers and white space characters. The scanf function can be used to enter and either store or discard as many data items as there are conversion specifiers in the control string. The specifiers can be separated by spaces or tabs to make them more legible but this is optional and can have a side effect which will be described later in the chapter. The control string has to be enclosed within quotes and the scanf conversion specifiers are not all the same as their equivalent printf conversion specifiers.

The scanf conversion specifiers

The scanf conversion specifiers

Identifier	Format
%d	integer, decimal notation
%i	integer in decimal, octal or hexadecimal notation
%c	character sequence, length determined by precision

%s	character sequence excluding white space characters
%f	floating point, decimal notation
%e	floating point, exponential notation
%g	floating point, either notation
%u	unsigned integer, decimal notation
%o	unsigned octal integer, without 0 prefix
%x	unsigned hexadecimal integer, without 0x prefix
%p	a hexadecimal address to be stored in a pointer
%n	number of characters read so far
%[...]	accept only the characters represented by ...
%[^...]	accept any characters except those represented by...

The scanf conversion specifiers use the following general form

```
% [*] [number] [modifier] character
```

The optional * is used to match and then discard any input type. The * means match the input type but do not make an assignment. There must not be a pointer argument corresponding to this conversion specifier because the input is discarded.

The optional integer decimal number (without a period prefix) is used to give the maximum number of characters accepted by scanf for a particular data item. This is most often used with the %c and %s specifiers.

The modifiers l (lower case L), L and h can be used to specify types long, long double and short respectively. These modifiers are mandatory if pointers to a specific type are used. If, for example, the argument points to a long double variable then the specifier in the control string must use either %Lf or %Le or %Lg. Pointers to long integers must use one of the specifiers %ld %li %lu %lo or %lx, pointers to double must use either %le %lf or %lg, and pointers to short integers must use one of the specifiers %hd %hi %hu %ho or %hx.

A specifier character is mandatory and can be any one of the conversion characters d, c, f, s, and so on.

Unlike printf, where a list of variable identifiers follows the control string, scanf requires a list of variable addresses, that is, pointers to variables, to follow the control string. The "address of" operator, &, can be used in front of a variable identifier to point to the address of that variable. If an integer variable cardinal is declared then &cardinal is the address of the first byte allocated to that variable, or a pointer to the variable cardinal. Remember that we cannot use variable identifiers with scanf, only pointers to variables.

The function scanf returns the number of fields read and the returned value can be used to check that all the required fields have been read. Because scanf is very fussy about the format of the data it reads a program often requires much more than just a simple check to make sure that scanf has worked as the programmer expects it to work.

The program scanfdemo demonstrates how to use pointers to variables with scanf. In this example the conversion specifier [...] specifies the four words yes no YES and NO with [yesnoYESNO]. Only these characters are acceptable as input.

```
/*
 * file name: scanfdemo
 * using pointers with scanf
 */

#include <stdio.h>
#include <stdlib.h>

#define empty_buffer while(getchar()!='\n'){}

int main(void)
  {
  char yes_no[20];
  int count, number;

  printf("Type either yes or no and press Return : ");
  count = scanf("%[yesnoYESNO] %n", yes_no, &number);
  empty_buffer
  printf("%d field(s) matched\n", count);
  printf("number = %d\n", number);
  printf("You typed %s\n", yes_no);
  exit(EXIT_SUCCESS);
  }
```

6.3.2 Problems with scanf

When scanf is used to read input from the keyboard it treats the contents of the keyboard buffer just as it would a machine formatted file. This makes scanf very inflexible and if the input does not match the conversion specifiers in every detail then scanf will abandon the input as soon as a mismatch is found. When the input is abandoned the result is that no value is assigned to the corresponding variable and very often data will be left in the input buffer ready to upset the next use of scanf. This dangerous tendency to leave unwanted characters in the input buffer can be tamed with routines such as empty_buffer as used in the program scanfdemo. The macro empty_buffer empties the keyboard buffer after scanf. Do not type a semicolon after using empty_buffer because the macro definition ends with a closing brace } which, in this case, is not followed with a semicolon.

The function scanf will also ignore white space characters with all conversion specifiers except %c. You can demonstrate some of the problems you can expect by executing the program compiled from scanfdemo and type a string of alpha-numeric characters not included in the conversion specifier.

These problems can be made much worse by increasing the number of data items to be read with scanf. This can be demonstrated with the program problems which is used to read three data items – an integer followed by a space, then a single character followed by another space and lastly a floating point number. If you execute this program and type, for example

```
123 a 123.456
```

then scanf will read and correctly assign the input to the appropriate variables. The spaces between the entered data items are used to indicate where one data item ends and another begins. Problems will arise if you execute the program and type

```
1.234
```

then scanf will still read three variables. The first data item will be the integer 1, the second data item will be the period character, and the last data item will be the integer 234 which scanf will convert to a floating point number. The function scanf will return the number 3 indicating that it has read the data as formatted.

```c
/*
 * file name: problems
 * make life difficult with scanf
 */

#include <stdio.h>
#include <stdlib.h>

int main(void)
  {
  void clear_buffer(void);
  int cardinal, count;
  char key;
  double decimal;

  printf("Type an integer, a space, a character,\n");
  printf("another space and a floating point number : ");
  count = scanf("%d %c %lf", &cardinal, &key, &decimal);
```

```
  clear_buffer();
  printf("%d field(s) matched\n", count);
  printf("You typed %d %c %lf\n", cardinal, key, decimal);
  exit(EXIT_SUCCESS);
  }

void clear_buffer(void)
  {
  char letter;

  while(letter = getchar(), letter != '\n')
    {
    printf("Emptying buffer of \'%c\'\n", letter);
    }
  return;
  }
```

The function scanf gets its name because it scans the input file trying to match every character in the buffer with its format specifiers as soon as the Return key or Enter key is pressed. Any number of scanf function calls may be made in a program and any number of data items may be read using a single scanf call but extreme caution has to be exercised with this function. As well as abandoning an input leaving data in the buffer when a mismatch is found it can also leave data in the buffer if a user types in more than the function expects to find. This data will remain in the buffer waiting to cause trouble with the next use of scanf. The program problems tries to overcome this potential hazard by emptying the keyboard buffer immediately after using scanf. The function clear_buffer empties the buffer and informs the user if it finds any characters in the buffer. This function is equivalent to the macro empty_buffer.

It might seem as if some of the problems caused by scanf can be controlled by ensuring that the keyboard buffer is always empty both before and after using scanf. This can be done by using routines such as empty_buffer and clear_buffer. Using these routines might seem like an attractive idea but in practice it is often better to use an alternative input function. The demonstration programs should show that everything will work properly if, and only if, the user types in exactly the format that scanf expects to find, but scanf becomes quite unreliable if the user deviates even slightly from the required format.

6.3.3 scanf and malloc

Reading character strings into memory reserved with malloc is demonstrated in the program string. The memory allocation function malloc is defined in stdlib.h and it allocates memory for the number of bytes passed to it as an argument. It returns a pointer to the first byte of the allocated memory. The memory reserved by malloc can be released by passing the pointer returned by malloc to the complementary function free.

The conversion specifier %39s used by scanf in the program string permits the input of a name of up to 39 characters. forty bytes are allocated by malloc to ensure that there is room for the null end-of-string marker byte.

```c
/*
 * file name: string
 * read a character string
 */

#include <stdio.h>
#include <stdlib.h>

int main(void)
  {
  char *name;
  int age, count;

  name = malloc(40);
  printf("Type your first name, a space, and age\n");
  count = scanf("%39s %d", name, &age);
  printf("%d field(s) matched\n", count);
  printf("%s you are %d years old\n", name, age);
  free(name);
  exit(EXIT_SUCCESS);
  }
```

Character strings, like any other data item, can be matched by scanf and then discarded. The program discard will match and then discard a character string (that is, up to the first white space character) and then match and assign an integer. A pointer to a character array must not be included in the list of pointers in scanf because the discarded character string is not assigned to a character array, or anything else, it is simply discarded.

```c
/*
 * file name: discard
 * match and discard a string
 */

#include <stdio.h>
#include <stdlib.h>
```

```
int main(void)
  {
  int age, count;

  printf("Type your first name, a space, and age\n");
  count = scanf("%*s %d", &age);
  printf("%d field(s) matched\n", count);
  printf("You are %d years old\n", age);
  exit(EXIT_SUCCESS);
  }
```

6.3.4 Text in the scanf control string

Any text included in the control string has to be typed in the input. The control string in the program 'today' expects the date to be typed with the days, months and years separated with the / symbol. The spaces in the control string do not have to typed when the date is entered. You could type the date as 24/10/1991 or 24 / 10 / 1991 and both will be accepted by scanf. If the control string is altered to read "%2d/%2d/%4d" then you can only use the format 24/10/1991. You need to be careful about including spaces in the control string because if you precede the single character conversion specifier %c with a space then only a space will be accepted for that character unless the space is used to terminate another data item. At other times white space characters in the control string are only used to improve the legibility of the source code.

```
/*
 * file name: today
 * data item separators
 */

#include <stdio.h>
#include <stdlib.h>

int main(void)
  {
  int day, month, year, count;

  printf("Type today's date (format dd/mm/yyyy) ");
  count = scanf("%2d / %2d / %4d", &day, &month, &year);
  printf("%d field(s) matched\n", count);
  printf("Today's date = %02d/%02d/%d\n", day, month,
     year);
  exit(EXIT_SUCCESS);
  }
```

6.4 Preferred functions for keyboard input

6.4.1 gets

The function gets is used to get a string from the standard input file, the keyboard. The general form of the function is

```
gets(pointer)
```

The pointer must point to a char array or to a reserved area of memory which is large enough to store the character string typed at the keyboard. If you fail to allocate sufficient memory for the character string you can expect to run into problems when the program is executing.

```
/*
 * file name: getstring
 * demonstrate the function gets
 */

#include <stdio.h>
#include <stdlib.h>

int main(void)
  {
  char string[100];

  printf("Type a character string : ");
  gets(string);
  printf("You typed: %s\n", string);
  exit(EXIT_SUCCESS);
  }
```

The program getstring will work properly as long as no more than 99 characters are typed. You need to have the spare character for a null end-of-string marker byte. The function inserts the null byte but the carriage return at the end of the string is not stored by gets.

The function gets is a simple input function to use but it can result in problems if the char array or reserved area of memory receiving the input is too small to store all the characters typed at the keyboard. There is related function in the stdio.h file which can be used to control this problem. It is called fgets and, because it offers more control than gets, it is just a little bit more complicated to use.

6.4.2 fgets

The function fgets has the following general form

```
fgets(pointer, number, stream)
```

The first argument is a pointer and, as with gets, this must point to a char array or reserved area of memory which is large enough to store the character string being entered. The second argument is the maximum number of characters in the input string.

The second argument should be an integer 1 less than the size of the receiving array. The function fgets reads up to number-1 characters from the input stream. This leaves one byte free for the carriage return character and another byte free for the null end-of-string marker byte before all the available memory is used.

The third argument is used to define the source of the input. The file stdio.h defines a number of external variables for standard input and output streams.

Stream	*Device*
stdin	keyboard
stdout	vdu
stdprn	printer
stderr	output device for error messages
stdaux	auxiliary port

The function fgets cannot take input from an output stream and so not all of the devices can be used in the third argument.

The program getstring can be modified to use fgets to take input from the keyboard and to make sure that only a fixed maximum number of characters are entered. In the following example 100 bytes of memory are reserved with the function malloc and released with the function free.

```
/*
 * file name: fgetstring
 * demonstrate the function fgets
 */

#include <stdio.h>
#include <stdlib.h>
```

```
int main(void)
  {
  char *string;

  string = malloc(100);
  printf("Type a character string : ");
  fgets(string, 99, stdin);
  printf("You typed: %s", string);
  free(string);
  exit(EXIT_SUCCESS);
  }
```

When either gets or fgets is used it will return a character string. If you want to use either of these functions to enter a number into a program then it is necessary to convert the character string into the appropriate variable type. One of a number of functions can be used to make this conversion. The easiest to use conversion functions are

atof	ASCII to floating point
atoi	ASCII to int
atol	ASCII to long

The program which used fgets to enter a character string can be modified to enter a floating point number. The conversion functions are defined in the file stdlib.h.

```
/*
 * file name: convert
 * demonstrate the functions fgets and atof
 */

#include <stdio.h>
#include <stdlib.h>

int main(void)
  {
  char *string;
  double answer;

  string = malloc(20);
  printf("Type a floating point number : ");
  fgets(string, 19, stdin);
  answer = atof(string);
  printf("You typed: %f", answer);
  free(string);
  exit(EXIT_SUCCESS);
  }
```

6.5 puts

The function puts is the complement of gets and it can be used to output a simple character string. The general form of puts is

```
puts(pointer)
```

The pointer points to a character string or char array. The function is very simple to use but it can only be used with character strings and not with variables. All character strings must end with a null end-of-string marker byte and the function puts automatically substitutes a new line character for the null byte when the string is displayed. The following example shows how puts can be used to print a simple message.

```
/*
 * file name: puts
 * demonstrate the function puts
 */

#include <stdio.h>
#include <stdlib.h>

int main(void)
  {
  static char message1[] = "This is the first message";
  char *message2 = "Now the second message";
  char message3[100];

  puts("Type your message ");
  gets(message3);
  puts(message1);
  puts(message2);
  puts("your message is: ");
  puts(message3);
  exit(EXIT_SUCCESS);
  }
```

6.6 getchar

The getchar function is used to read a single character from the input stream. The function returns the value of the character and the character is echoed on the VDU screen. The function has no argument and it waits for the Return key or Enter key to be pressed before returning. If more than one character is typed before pressing the Return key then only the first character is returned by getchar.

```
/*
 * file name: getchar
 * demonstrate the function getchar
 */

#include <stdio.h>
#include <stdlib.h>

int main(void)
  {
  char letter;

  printf("Type a single character : ");
  letter = getchar();
  printf("You typed: %c\n", letter);
  exit(EXIT_SUCCESS);
  }
```

The function printf in this example could be replaced with the function putchar which is the complement of getchar.

6.7 putchar

putchar is used to output a single character. The general form of putchar is

```
putchar(character)
```

The last line of the program used to illustrate getchar could be replaced with

```
putchar(letter);
```

Because putchar takes a single character as an argument and getchar returns a single character, getchar can be used as the argument for putchar. For example

```
putchar(getchar())
```

will get a character from the standard input file (the keyboard) and display it on the standard output file (the VDU screen).

```
/*
 * file name: putchar
 * demonstrate the functions getchar and putchar
 */

#include <stdio.h>
#include <stdlib.h>

int main(void)
  {
  char letter;

  printf("Type a single character\n");
  letter = getchar();
  printf("You typed: ");
  putchar(letter);
  printf("\n");
  exit(EXIT_SUCCESS);
  }
```

7

Operators

7.1 Operators and operands

Operators are used to perform actions. An operator defines the action that is to be performed on one or more operands. An operator operates on the operands.

In the following expression the characters * / + - and = are operators.

```
a = b * c / d + e - f
```

The variables a, b, c, d, e and f are operands. When an expression such as the one above is followed with a semicolon it is no longer described as an expression, it then becomes a C statement.

There are over 40 operators in C and many of the operators, such as * / + - and =, will be familiar to BASIC programmers but there are other operators, such as ++ -- *= and -=, which will be new to some programmers.

The operators used by C can be thought of as belonging to one of six groups: assignment, arithmetic, special, bitwise, logical and relational. Logical and relational operators are mainly used to control the flow in a program and these operators are described in chapter eight. The first four groups of operators are dealt with in this chapter.

7.2 The assignment operator

The assignment operator is represented by the equal sign. The assignment operator takes the value of the expression to the right of the equal sign and assigns that value to the variable on the left of the equal sign. For example

```
x = 1.23;
y = z;
```

The general form of the assignment operator is

```
l_value = expression
```

Error messages generated by the compiler often refer to the variable to the left of the assignment operator as the l_value, as in the general form above, rather than the variable identifier, x or y or whatever is used in the source code. The compiler error message "l_value required" usually means that the left hand side of an assignment operator is lacking a suitable variable identifier.

In C, we can make multiple assignments in a single statement. For example

```
x = y = 1.23;
```

is perfectly legal if both x and y are double precision variables. The statement assigns the value 1.23 to both x and y. It is important not to confuse the assignment operator = with the equality operator ==. The reserved word == is used to mean "is equal to" and != is used to mean "is not equal to". You cannot use, for example, (x = y) in a conditional statement to mean "x is equal to y", you must use (x == y).

7.3 Arithmetic operators

There are six arithmetic operators which are evaluated with the following priority

Arithmetic Operator	Meaning	Priority
+	unary plus (positive)	high priority
−	unary minus (negative)	
*	multiply	
/	divide	middle priority
%	integer remainder	
+	add	
−	subtract	low priority

Unary plus and minus perform an operation with one operand. The others perform an action with two operands. The operands can be constants or variables. For example, using the add operator:

```
x = y + 1.2;
```

the value of (y + 1.2) is assigned to x.

The arithmetic operators can be a part of a function argument. For example, using the subtract operator

```
printf("%f\n", 3.4 - 1.2);
```

will print 2.200000, the difference between 3.4 and 1.2

The unary plus and minus operators should not be confused with the add and subtract operators. Unary minus takes one operand and forces the operand to take a negative value. For example

```
x = -10;
```

the value of minus 10 is assigned to the variable x. The unary plus operator is available but largely redundant because an operand is positive by default.

The integer remainder operator can only be used for integer arithmetic. It provides the remainder when the left operand is divided by the right operand. For example

```
printf("%d\n", 13 % 3);
```

will print the value 1 because 13 divided by 3 leaves a remainder of 1. The quotient can be obtained with divide operator. The use of the divide operator / is common to both integers and floating point numbers although the results obtained are not always what might be expected. The value assigned to the following operations depends on the data type of the operands. If there are any floating point operands then the value assigned to the operation is floating point. An integer value is only assigned to an operation when all the operands are integer type.

13 / 3	is equal to 4	integer operands
13. / 3	is equal to 4.333	mixed integer and floating point
13. / 3.	is equal to 4.333	floating point operands

The order in which the operators are evaluated can be altered by using parentheses. Parentheses have a higher priority than all the operators and they are used to force a priority over operators. For example, the statement

```
x = 1.0 + 20.0 / 2.0 * 5.0;
```

is evaluated as divide 20.0 by 2.0, then multiply this number by 5.0 and then add 1.0 to the result, so that x is assigned the value 51.0. This statement is equivalent to:

```
x = 1.0 + ((20.0 / 2.0) * 5.0);
```

But the priority can be altered with parentheses, for example

```
x = (1.0 + 20.0) / 2.0 * 5.0;
```

Now the expression is evaluated as add 1.0 and 20.0, divide this number by 2.0, and then multiply the result by 5.0, so that x is assigned the value 52.5.

Because the evaluation of an expression depends on the priority of the operators it is often a good idea to use parentheses to give explicit control over the evaluation of an expression.

```
/*
 * file name: prior
 * alter priority with parentheses
 */

#include <stdio.h>
#include <stdlib.h>

int main(void)
  {
  double x;

  x = 1.0 + 20.0 / 2.0 * 5.0;
  printf("1.0 + 20.0 / 2.0 * 5.0 = %f\n", x);
  x = 1.0 + ((20.0 / 2.0) * 5.0);
  printf("1.0 + ((20.0 / 2.0) * 5.0) = %f\n", x);
  x = (1.0 + 20.0) / 2.0 * 5.0;
  printf("(1.0 + 20.0) / 2.0 * 5.0 = %f\n", x);
  exit(EXIT_SUCCESS);
  }
```

7.4 Special operators

There are several special operators used in C including the increment and decrement operators, the arithmetic assignment operators, the cast operator, the sizeof operator, the comma operator and pointer related operators. Pointer related operators are examined in chapter ten.

7.4.1 Increment and decrement operators

The increment and decrement operators are used to simplify the addition and subtraction of unit quantities.

```
x = y++;
```

is equivalent to

```
x = y;
y = y + 1;
```

and

```
a = ++b;
```

is equivalent to

```
b = b + 1;
a = b;
```

In the first case, x = y++, x is incremented by 1 after the assignment takes place. In the second case, a = ++b, b is incremented by one before the assignment takes place. The decrement operator works in the same way as the increment operator.

```
x = y--;
```

is equivalent to

```
x = y;
y = y - 1;
```

and

```
a = --b;
```

is equivalent to

```
b = b - 1;
a = b;
```

In the first case, x = y--, x is decremented by 1 after the assignment takes place and in the second case, a = --b, b is decremented by one before the assignment takes place.

The use of the increment and decrement operators is demonstrated in the program increment

```
/*
 * file name: increment
 * demonstrate the increment and decrement operators
 */

#include <stdio.h>
#include <stdlib.h>

int main(void)
  {
  int x = 3;
  int y = 6;

  printf("x = %d, y = %d\n", x, y);
  puts("perform x = y++");
  x = y++;
  printf("x = %d, y = %d\n", x, y);
  puts("perform x = ++y");
  x = ++y;
  printf("x = %d, y = %d\n", x, y);
  puts("perform x = y--");
  x = y--;
  printf("x = %d, y = %d\n", x, y);
  puts("perform x = --y");
  x = --y;
  printf("x = %d, y = %d\n", x, y);
  exit(EXIT_SUCCESS);
  }
```

The increment and decrement operators are frequently used in for loops to alter the value of the control variable. These operators produce very efficient code and they should always be used whenever they are appropriate.

7.4.2 Arithmetic assignment operators

In C, the arithmetic assignment

```
x += 10;
```

is equivalent to

```
x = x + 10;
```

and

```
x -= y;
```

is equivalent to

```
x = x - y;
```

All the arithmetic assignment operators follow the same pattern as the above examples.

x += y	is equivalent to	x = x + y
x -= y	is equivalent to	x = x - y
x *= y	is equivalent to	x = x * y
x /= y	is equivalent to	x = x / y
x %= y	is equivalent to	x = x % y

There are similar bitwise assignment operators and these will be dealt with later in this chapter.

7.4.3 The cast operator

The cast operator is used to force a change in the data type of a variable. Casting can be explicit or implicit. Explicit casting involves putting the type in parentheses before the variable in an expression. For example

```
/*
 * file name: castop
 * demonstrate the cast operator
 */

#include <stdio.h>
#include <stdlib.h>

int main(void)
  {
  char c;
  int i;
  float f;
  double d = 65.0;
  c = (char) d;
  i = (int) (d / 2.0);
  f = (float) (d * d);
  printf("65.0 cast to char gives : %c\n", c);
```

```
printf("(65.0 / 2.0) cast to int gives : %d\n", i);
printf("(65.0 squared) cast to float gives : %f\n", f);
exit(EXIT_SUCCESS);
}
```

Implicit casting

Implicit casting, also known as type conversion, occurs when variable types are mixed in an expression. In the following outline program the integer value of i is cast into a double precision floating point value and then multiplied by the double precision variable d. The result is assigned to the double precision floating point variable f.

```
int main(void)
  {
  int i = 2;
  double d = 3.0;
  double f;

  f = i * d;
  }
```

The rules controlling type conversion are quite complicated but they can be summarised by assuming there is a hierarchy of data types with long double at the top of the hierarchy and int at the bottom.

Type conversion hierarchy

high	long double	
	double	
	float	
	unsigned long	
	long	
	int	unsigned int
	short	unsigned short
	unsigned char	
low	char	

Rule 1

Data types short, unsigned char and char are cast to type int and unsigned short is cast to unsigned int if type conversion is necessary. This is known as integer promotion.

Rule 2

Type conversion is applied to pairs of operands as they are evaluated to ensure that the types of any two operands being evaluated in an expression will be the same. A data type lower in the hierarchy is promoted to a data type higher in the hierarchy to ensure that the two data types are the same.

It's a good idea to avoid using implicit casting. Explicit casting gives much clearer control over the variables in a program.

7.4.4 The size of operator

This operator returns the number of bytes used to store its operand and it can be used with a variable, a constant or a data type. The program sizeof demonstrates the use of the sizeof operator by printing the number of bytes used for each data type.

```
/*
 * file name: sizeof
 * demonstrate the use of the sizeof operator
 */

#include <stdio.h>
#include <stdlib.h>

int main(void)
  {
  printf("The size of char %d bytes\n", sizeof(char));
  printf("the size of short %d bytes\n", sizeof(short));
  printf("the size of int %d bytes\n", sizeof(int));
  printf("the size of long %d bytes\n", sizeof(long));
  printf("the size of float %d bytes\n", sizeof(float));
  printf("the size of double %d bytes\n", sizeof(double));
  printf("and long double %d bytes\n", sizeof(long
     double));
  exit(EXIT_SUCCESS);
  }
```

7.4.5 The comma operator

Two expressions separated by a comma operator form a comma expression. The general form of a comma expression is

```
expression1 , expression2
```

The expression represented by expression1 is evaluated first followed by expression2 and the value assigned to the whole comma expression is equal to that of expression2.

The comma operator is demonstrated in the program comma. In this program the value of the comma expression is either true or false and this value is used to control the while loop. A modified version of this program is used in chapter six to ensure that the keyboard buffer is empty after using the input function scanf.

```
/*
 * file name: comma
 * demonstrate the comma operator
 */

#include <stdio.h>
#include <stdlib.h>

int main(void)
  {
  char key;

  printf("Type something into the keyboard buffer\n");
  while (key = getchar() , key != '\n')
    {
    printf("%c", key);
    }
  printf("\nbuffer empty\n");
  exit(EXIT_SUCCESS);
  }
```

7.5 Bitwise operators

The bitwise operators provided by C are used to manipulate the bit patterns which make up the representation of all the data stored within a computer's memory and they can be used to extract the information stored in the individual bits of registers, pseudo-registers or flag variables. The bits in a flag variable represent on/off states and the information is usually extracted by ANDing the flag with a bit mask. This isolates and identifies the required bit(s).

The source code of a C program cannot directly specify the binary representation of an integer. In some other languages a binary number such as 01111011 can be prefixed with the % symbol to indicate that the 0s and 1s are used to form the binary representation of an integer. In C you can only use either octal (base 8), denary (base 10) or hexadecimal (base 16) representations of an integer. Octal numbers are represented by prefixing the number with a zero, for example 0177 or 023. Denary numbers are represented by the integer without a prefix and hexadecimal numbers are prefixed with 0x, for example 0xFF or 0x1234.

The binary number 01111011 will usually be represented as denary 123 or hexadecimal 73 (0x73) in the source code of a program. In this chapter the binary representations of numbers are used to explain how the bitwise operators work because using a binary representation make the concepts much easier to understand. It is important to remember that this use of binary numbers is just a symbolic pseudo-code and we cannot use the binary representations of numbers in C source code.

Although the source code of a C program cannot cope with the binary representations of numbers, the input to and output from a C program is completely under its programmer's control and two programs later in this chapter will show just how easy it is to use the bitwise operators provided by C to achieve binary input and output.

There are six bitwise operators, and five of these bitwise operators can be combined with the = symbol to provide bitwise assignment operators.

Bitwise *Operator*	*Meaning*
&	bitwise AND
|	bitwise inclusive OR
^	bitwise exclusive OR (XOR)
~	bitwise NOT
<< n	shift left, n bits
>> n	shift right, n bits

Bitwise *Assignment* *Operator*	*Meaning*
&=	bitwise AND and assign
|=	bitwise inclusive OR and assign
^=	bitwise exclusive OR and assign
<<= n	bitwise shift right n bits and assign
>>= n	bitwise shift left n bits and assign

The programs which demonstrate the bitwise operators and bitwise assignment operators all use 8 bit numbers stored in char variables. The techniques demonstrated in the following programs can also be used with 32 bit integers. 8 bit numbers are only used to keep the binary representations of the numbers reasonably short.

7.5.1 AND

The bitwise AND operator & produces a 1 in the corresponding output bit position if, and only if, both the input bits in that position are 1. There is no carry. Symbolically

10101010 & 00001111 = 00001010 or in denary 170 & 15 = 10

Using C

```
/*
 * file name: bitand
 * demonstrate bitwise AND
 */

#include <stdio.h>
#include <stdlib.h>

int main(void)
  {
  char result = 170;
  char mask = 15;

  result = result & mask; /* result &= mask */
  printf("170 & 15 = %d\n", result);
  exit(EXIT_SUCCESS);
  }
```

The printf function will print the result 10 because 170 & 15 = 10.

7.5.2 Inclusive OR

The bitwise inclusive OR operator | produces a 1 in the corresponding output bit position if either of the input bits in that position are 1. Symbolically

10101010 | 00001111 = 10101111 or in denary 170 | 15 = 175

Using C

```
/*
 * file name: bitor
 * demonstrate bitwise inclusive OR
 */
```

```
#include <stdio.h>
#include <stdlib.h>

int main(void)
  {
  char result = 170;
  char mask = 15;

  result = result | mask; /* result |= mask */
  printf("170 | 15 = %d\n", result);
  exit(EXIT_SUCCESS);
  }
```

The printf function will print the result 175 because 170 & 15 = 175.

7.5.3 Exclusive OR

The bitwise exclusive OR operator ^ produces a 1 in the corresponding bit position if either of the input bits in that position are 1, but it produces a 0 if both bits are 1 or both bits are 0. Symbolically

10101010 ^ 00001111 = 10100101 or in denary 170 ^ 15 = 165

Using C

```
/*
 * file name: bitxor
 * demonstrate bitwise exclusive OR
 */

#include <stdio.h>
#include <stdlib.h>

int main(void)
  {
  char result = 170;
  char mask = 15;
  result = result ^ mask; /* result ^= mask */
  printf("170 ^ 15 = %d\n", result);
  exit(EXIT_SUCCESS);
  }
```

The printf function will print the result 10 because 170 ^ 15 = 165.

7.5.4 NOT

The bitwise NOT operator ~, sometimes known as the complement or the one's complement, changes each 0 to 1 and each 1 to 0. Symbolically

~10101010 = 01010101 or in denary ~170 = 85

and

~11111111 = 00000000 or NOT true = false

Using C

```
/*
 * file name: bitnot
 * demonstrate bitwise NOT
 */

#include <stdio.h>
#include <stdlib.h>

int main(void)
  {
  char result = 170;
  result = ~result;
  printf("~170 = %d\n", result);
  exit(EXIT_SUCCESS);
  }
```

The printf function will print the result 85 because ~170 = 85.

7.5.5 Left Shift

The left shift operator <<n shifts the bits of the left operand to the left by the number of space specified by the right operand. The left bits are lost and the right bits are filled with zeros. Symbolically

11111111 << 2 = 11111100 or in denary 255 << 2 = 252

and

11111111 << 4 = 11110000 or in denary 255 << 4 = 240

Using C

```
/*
 * file name: leftshift
 * demonstrate left shift
 */

#include <stdio.h>
#include <stdlib.h>

int main(void)
  {
  char result = 255;

  result = result << 2; /* result <<= 2 */
  printf("255 << 2 = %d\n", result);
  exit(EXIT_SUCCESS);
  }
```

The printf function will print the result 252 because 255 << 2 = 252.

7.5.6 Right Shift

The right shift operator >>n shifts the bits of the left operand to the right by the number of space specified by the right operand. The right bits are lost and the left bits are filled with zeros. Symbolically

11111111 >> 2 = 00111111 or in denary 255 >> 2 = 63

and

11111111 >> 4 = 00001111 or in denary 255 >> 4 = 15

Using C

```
/*
 * file name: rtshift
 * demonstrate right shift
 */

#include <stdio.h>
#include <stdlib.h>

int main(void)
  {
  char result = 255;
```

```
result = result >> 2; /* result >>= 2 */
printf("255 >> 2 = %d\n", result);
exit(EXIT_SUCCESS);
}
```

The printf function will print the result 63 because 255 >> 2 = 63.

The example programs bitand, bitor, bitxor, leftshift and rtshift can all use a bitwise assignment operator and have the alternative operator described within comments. For example

result = result >> 2 is equivalent to result >>= 2

and

result = result & mask is equivalent to result &= mask

The truth table below summarises the rules which are applied to the use of the AND, Inclusive OR and Exclusive OR (XOR) bitwise operators.

First Operand	Second Operand	AND &	OR /	XOR ^
0	0	0	0	0
0	1	0	1	1
1	0	0	1	1
1	1	1	1	0

The left and right shift operators can be used to perform two integer arithmetic operations. The left shift operator can be used to multiply an integer by two for every shift left, and the right shift operator can divide an integer by two (and lose the remainder) for every shift right.

A common use for bitwise operators is to mask the unwanted bits in a flag byte. This is done by first producing a mask byte with 1s stored in the bits that are significant in the flag byte. Then AND the mask byte with the flag byte. All the unwanted bits become zero and all the significant bits retain their original value.

If, for example, we are interested in the status of bit 3 in a flag byte then the mask byte will store the binary number 00001000 (denary 8). When the mask byte is ANDed with flag byte the result is 8 if bit 3 of the flag byte is 1 and 0 if bit 3 of the flag byte is zero. All the other bits are ignored.

The use of bitwise operators is further illustrated in the two demonstration programs bin2int and int2bin. The first of these programs converts an eight bit binary input into a decimal integer and the second performs the reverse operation. Compile and link

both programs and then either double click on the application icon or, in response to
the command line prompt, type

```
bin2int 10101010
```

and

```
int2bin 170
```

The first program will convert the binary number 10101010 into the denary
equivalent 170, and the second program will perform the reverse operation converting
the denary number 170 into the binary equivalent 10101010.

```
/*
 * file name: bin2int
 * convert binary to integer
 */

#include <stdio.h>
#include <string.h>
#include <stdlib.h>

int main(int argc, char *argv[])
   {
   int bitmask, loop, length;
   int answer = 0;
   static char binary[20];
if (argc != 2)
   {
   printf("Enter binary number : ");
   gets(binary);
   }
else strcpy(binary, argv[1]);
length = strlen(binary);
if (length > 8)
   {
   puts("No more than 8 bits");
   exit(EXIT_FAILURE);
   }
for (loop = 0; loop < length; loop++)
   {
   answer <<= 1;
   switch (binary[loop])
      {
```

```
      case '0':
        {
        bitmask = 0;
        break;
        }
      case '1':
        {
        bitmask = 1;
        break;
        }
      default:
        {
        puts("Use binary argument");
        exit(EXIT_FAILURE);
        }
      }
      answer |= bitmask;
   }
printf("%s = %d\n", binary, answer);
exit(EXIT_SUCCESS);
}

/*
 * file name: int2bin
 * convert integer to binary
 */

#include <stdio.h>
#include <stdlib.h>

int main(int argc, char *argv[])
  {
  int number, bit;
  int bitmask = 0x80;
  int loop;
  static char answer[10], buffer[10];

  if (argc != 2)
    {
    printf("Enter integer (0-255) : ");
    gets(buffer);
    number = atoi(buffer);
    }
```

```
  else number = atoi(argv[1]);
  if (number > 255)
    {
    puts("range 0-255 only");
    exit(EXIT_FAILURE);
    }
  printf("%d = ", number);
  for (loop = 0; loop < 8; loop++)
    {
    bit = number & bitmask;
    answer[loop] = (char) ((bit / bitmask) + 48);
    number <<= 1;
    }
  printf("%s\n", answer);
  exit(EXIT_SUCCESS);
  }
```

7.6 The precedence of operators

The precedence of an operator establishes its priority relative to all the other operators. In an expression with multiple operators, the operator with the highest precedence is used before an operator with a lower precedence. In an expression with multiple operators of the same precedence, the operators are evaluated according to their associativity. This means that evaluation is normally from left to right except for unary operators, the ?: operator (used in conditional expressions) and for the assignment operators which associate from right to left.

Precedence	Associativity	Type	Operators
15	L-R	Primary	( ) [ ] –> .
14	R-L	Unary	! ~ ++ –– + – (type) * & sizeof
13	L-R	Arithmetic	* / %
12	L-R	Arithmetic	+ –
11	L-R	Shift	> <
10	L-R	Relational	> >= < <=
9	L-R	Equality	== !=
8	L-R	Bitwise	&
7	L-R	Bitwise	^
6	L-R	Bitwise		
5	L-R	Logical	&&
4	L-R	Logical	‖
3	R-L	Conditional	?:
2	R-L	Assignment	= += –= *= /= %= > < &= ^= |=
1	L-R	Comma	,

Precedence can be controlled using parentheses. Because parentheses are in the group with the highest precedence they can be used to raise the precedence of any of the other operators in an expression. The precedence of operators is described in more detail in appendix two.

Program control

8.1 Logical and relational operators

Logical operators are used to test for either true or false conditions in conditional statements. Expressions using logical operators always produce a result that is either true or false. By convention false is equal to 0 and true is equal to -1 but C breaks away from this tradition and represents true by the integer 1, although any non zero integer including -1 is also recognized as true. Logical operators can be used with relational operators and other operators to create expressions and statements.

There are three logical operators AND, OR and NOT. There are equivalent bitwise operators with the same names as these three operators but we must always be careful to use the correct operator for the job the program is doing. We must always use logical operators for logical decision making and bitwise operators for bit manipulation and never confuse logical and bitwise operators, they may have similar names but they have different symbols and slightly different actions.

These are the three logical operators.

Logical Operator	Meaning
&&	logical AND
||	logical inclusive OR
!	logical NOT

There are two equality operators and a further four relational operators which are used for making logical comparisons.

Equality Operator	Meaning
==	is equal to
!=	is not equal to

Relational Operator Meaning

>	is greater than
<	is less than
>=	is greater than or equal to
<=	is less than or equal to

These operators are used in conditional expressions to selectively direct the flow of control in a program. The if-else conditional statement is common to most high level languages and it is also used in C. The general form of this statement in C is

```
if (conditional_expression)
  {
  /* statements executed if conditional_expression is
   true */
  }
else
  {
  /* statements executed if conditional_expression is
   false */
  }
```

All the logical operators produce the result true or false. It can be useful to have both true and false defined as macros. We should use the preprocessor to check that true and false have not been defined by C before defining them ourself. This can be done with the following preprocessor commands

```
#if !defined(TRUE)
  #define TRUE 1
  #define FALSE 0
#endif
```

If it is our intention to write portable C source code then we cannot assume that true and false are undefined just because they are not defined in the version we are using. We should always include the conditional definition, it does not make the application code any longer and it prevents a multiple and possibly conflicting definition of true. If true is defined as -1 in an included header file we cannot redefine it as 1 without first undefining the original definition. Using the above code will simply avoid this sort of complication.

8.1.1 AND

An expression using the logical AND operator && returns the result true if both the left hand and the right hand operand are true, otherwise it returns the result false.

```
/*
 * file name: logand
 * demonstrate logical AND
 */

#include <stdio.h>
#include <stdlib.h>

#if !defined(TRUE)
  #define TRUE 1
  #define FALSE 0
#endif

int main(void)
  {
  int left = TRUE;
  int right = TRUE;

  if (left && right)
    {
    puts("(%d AND %d) is true", left, right);
    }
  else
    {
    puts("(%d AND %d) is false", left, right);
    }
  exit(EXIT_SUCCESS);
  }
```

The program logand will print the result "(1 AND 1) is true" because both the variables left and right are assigned the value true. If the value false is assigned to the variable right then the program will print the result "(1 AND 0) is false".

8.1.2 OR

An expression using the logical OR operator || returns the result true if either the left hand or the right hand operand are true, or if both are true, otherwise it returns the result false.

```
/*
 * file name: logor
 * demonstrate logical OR
 */
```

```
#include <stdio.h>
#include <stdlib.h>

#if !defined(TRUE)
  #define TRUE 1
  #define FALSE 0
#endif

int main(void)
  {
  int left = TRUE;
  int right = FALSE;

  if (left || right)
    {
    puts("(%d OR %d) is true", left, right);
    }
  else
    {
    puts("(%d OR %d) is false", left, right);
    }
  exit(EXIT_SUCCESS);
  }
```

The program logor will print the result "(1 OR 0) is true" because the variable left is
assigned the value true. The only way to get the program to indicate a false result is
to assign the value false to both the variables left and right.

8.1.3 NOT

Logical NOT ! is a unary operator and only requires one operand. NOT true is always
false and NOT false is always true.

```
/*
 * file name: lognot
 * demonstrate logical NOT
 */

#include <stdio.h>
#include <stdlib.h>

#if !defined(TRUE)
  #define TRUE 1
```

```
      #define FALSE 0
#endif

int main(void)
   {
   int value = FALSE;

   if (!value) puts("(NOT false) is true");
   else puts("(NOT false) is false");
   exit(EXIT_SUCCESS);
   }
```

The program lognot will print the result "(NOT false) is true".

The equality and relational operators can be used in the if-else construction in the same way as the logical operators are used. For example

```
/*
 * file name: ifelse
 * demonstrate equality operator in if-else
 */

#include <stdio.h>
#include <stdlib.h>

#if !defined(TRUE)
   #define TRUE 1
   #define FALSE 0
#endif

int main(void)
   {
   int left = TRUE;
   int right = FALSE;

   if (left != right) /* if left is not equal to right */
     {
     puts("true is not equal to false");
     }
   else
     {
     puts("true is equal to false");
```

```
    }
  exit(EXIT_SUCCESS);
    }
```

The program ifelse will print the result "true is not equal to false" because the expression (left != right) evaluates as true. Any of the equality and relational operators can be used in the same way to test whether a condition is either true or false. These operators only produce the result true or false and the result can be assigned to other variables. For example

```
/*
 * file name: assign
 * assign the result of a comparison to a variable
 */

#include <stdio.h>
#include <stdlib.h>

#if !defined(TRUE)
  #define TRUE 1
  #define FALSE 0
#endif

int main(void)
  {
  int left = TRUE;
  int right = FALSE;
  int answer;

  answer = (left == right);
  printf("value assigned to (true == false) is %d\n"
    answer);
  exit(EXIT_SUCCESS);
  }
```

In this case the expression (left == right) evaluates to false because the variable left is not equal to the variable right. The false result is assigned to the variable answer and the program will print "value assigned to (true == false) is 0".

8.2 Decisions

There are two reserved words used to make decisions in C. These reserved words are if and switch. The reserved word if may or may not be associated with the reserved word else but the reserved word switch is always associated with the reserved word case.

The most simple use of the if statement adopts the following general form

```
if (conditional_expression)
   {
   /* statements executed if conditional_expression is true */
   }
```

This form is read as "if the conditional expression is true then execute the statements within the braces, if the conditional expression is false then do not execute the statements within the braces". The conditional expression can be summarized as any expression that evaluates to give a true (non-zero) or a false (zero) result.

When a single statement is to executed as a result of the test the general form described above can be reduced to one line of source code.

```
   if (conditional_expression) statement;
```

This form can be used with a single statement but it's worth remembering that excluding the braces which define a block of code does not make the application file any smaller.

The reserved word else can be associated with the reserved word if in the following general form

```
   if (conditional_expression)
      {
      /* statements executed if conditional_expression is
      true */
      }
   else
      {
      /* statements executed if conditional_expression is
      false */
      }
```

Again this form can be abbreviated if only a single statement is to be executed as a result of the test. The one line form of if-else is

```
   if (conditional_expression) statement_true; else
      statement_false;
```

ANSI C provides an abbreviated alternative syntax for if-else which should appeal to those who are keen on cryptic coding.

```
conditional_expression ? expression_1 : expression_2;
```

Using C

```
/*
 * file name: abbrev
 * demonstrate abbreviated if-else
 */

#include <stdio.h>
#include <stdlib.h>

int main(void)
  {
  int cardinal = -10;

  printf("before, cardinal = %d\n", cardinal);
  cardinal = (cardinal < 0) ? -cardinal : cardinal;
  printf("after, cardinal = %d\n", cardinal);
  exit(EXIT_SUCCESS);
  }
```

The statement

```
cardinal = (cardinal < 0) ? -cardinal : cardinal;
```

can be read as "if the variable cardinal is less then zero then cardinal is assigned the value of minus cardinal, else cardinal is assigned the value cardinal". This statement is equivalent to

```
if (cardinal < 0)
  {
  cardinal = -cardinal;
  }
else
  {
  cardinal = cardinal;
  }
```

The conditional expression in the program abbrev is (cardinal < 0). If the conditional expression is true then the value of the expression to the left of the colon is assigned to the variable cardinal, if the conditional expression is false then the value of the expression to the right of the colon is assigned to the variable cardinal.

As well as appealing to cryptic coders the abbreviated forms of if-else can be very useful when defining macro instructions. This is because macro instructions are normally defined in just one line of code. Defining macro instructions is examined in chapter three.

8.2.1 Nested if statements

A series of if-else statements can be nested and/or chained. An if-else statement can contain any valid C statement including another if-else statement. Nested if statements can be created as shown below

```
if (expression_1)
   {
   if (expression_2) statement_1;
   }
else
   statement_2;
```

This nested if-else construction should be read as follows "if expression_1 is true then evaluate expression_2 and if expression_2 is also true then execute statement_1 but if expression_1 is false then execute statement_2".

The braces around the inner if statement are essential to produce nested if-else statements. Leaving out the braces completely alters the meaning of the statement.

```
if (expression_1)
   if (expression_2) statement_1;
   else statement_2;
```

Leaving out the braces will pair the else with the second if so that the construction is now read as "if expression_1 is true then evaluate expression_2 and if expression_2 is also true the execute statement_1 but if expression_2 is false then execute statement_2". If expression_1 is false then neither statement_1 nor statement_2 will be executed. The else is always paired with the closest unpaired if unless braces are used to alter the default pairing.

8.2.2 Chained if statements

In general, the use of nested if-else statements is confusing and best avoided whenever possible. The use of chained if-else statements is a lot less confusing. A

chained if-else statement occurs when the else part of an if-else statement contains
another if-else statement.

```
if (expression_1) statement_1;
else if (expression_2) statement_2;
    else statement_3;
```

This if-else chain is read as "if expression_1 is true then execute statement_1 but if
expression_1 is false then evaluate expression_2 and if expression_2 is true then
execute statement_2 but if expression_2 is false execute statement_3". Each
expression in the chain is evaluated in order and if an expression is true then the
corresponding statement is executed and the remainder of the chain is not evaluated.
The final statement associated with the last else in the chain is only executed if all the
expressions associated with the previous ifs are false. The chain can be as long as you
need to make it and each statement can be a compound statement surrounded by
braces.

The simple if-else construction can be considered as the programming equivalent of a
two way selector and an if-else chain is one way of creating the logical equivalent of
a multi-way selector. If all the conditional expressions within an if-else chain evaluate
to give either a char or an integer result then the if-else chain can be replaced with the
switch-case construction.

8.2.3 Switch and case

Although it is possible to use a chain of if-else statements to produce the equivalent
of a multi-way selector, you should find that using switch-case is neater and much
easier to understand. The reserved word switch is always associated with the reserved
word case and they are used together in the following general form

```
switch (integer_expression)
  {
  case 1:
    {
    statement_1;
    break;
    }
  case 2:
    {
    statement_2;
    break;
    }
  case n:
```

```
   {
   statement_n;
   break;
   }
 default:
   {
   default_statement;
   break;
   }
 }
```

When the switch statement is executed the expression in brackets following the keyword switch is evaluated and must give an integer or character result. The switch-case construction then attempts to match the result of the evaluation with the cases labelled case 1: case 2: and so on.

For example, if the integer_expression evaluates to integer 2 and statement_2 is associated with the label case 2: then statement_2 will be executed. If the label case 2: is not included in the list of cases then the statement associated with the label default: will be executed. The default statement is executed for all cases which do not match a specific case. The reserved word break can be used to jump out of the list of cases as soon as the statements selected by case have been executed. Using break is optional but highly desirable.

The demonstration program trig uses the switch-case construction to evaluate the sine and cosine of a number expressed in radians as well as the constant e (2.718...) raised to the power of that number.

The values of sine, cosine and e to the power of x are all calculated at the same time using the following related series.

$$\sin x = \frac{x}{1!} - \frac{x^3}{3!} + \frac{x^5}{5!} - \frac{x^7}{7!} + \dots$$

$$\cos x = 1 - \frac{x^2}{2!} + \frac{x^4}{4!} - \frac{x^6}{6!} + \dots$$

$$e^x = 1 + \frac{x}{1!} + \frac{x^2}{2!} + \frac{x^3}{3!} + \frac{x^4}{4!} + \dots$$

The program trig can be executed by double clicking on the application file icon or by typing, For example

```
   trig 0.5
```

The program will respond by printing the sine of 0.5 radians, the cosine of 0.5 radians and the value of e raised to the power of 0.5.

```c
/*
 * file name: trig
 * calculate trigonometric functions
 */

#include <stdio.h>
#include <stdlib.h>
#include <string.h>

int main(int argc, char *argv[])
  {
  double sine, power, etox, part, x;
  double cosine = 1.0;
  double factorial = 1.0;
  register int loop;
  char buffer[20];

  if (argc != 2)
    {
    printf("Enter x : ");
    gets(buffer);
    x = atof(buffer);
    }
  else
    {
    x = atof(argv[1]);
    strcpy(buffer, argv[1]);
    }
  sine = x;
  power = x;
  etox = 1.0 + x;
  for (loop=2; loop <= 30; loop++)
    {
    factorial *= (double) loop;
    power *= x;
    part = power/factorial;
    etox += part;
    switch (loop % 4)
      {
```

```
    case 0:
      {
      cosine += part;
      break;
      }
    case 1:
      {
      sine += part;
      break;
      }
    case 2:
      {
      cosine -= part;
      break;
      }
    case 3:
      {
      sine -= part;
      break;
      }
    default:
      {
      puts("Error !!!");
      exit(EXIT_FAILURE);
      }
    }
  }
printf("sin(%s) = %f\n", buffer, sine);
printf("cos(%s) = %f\n", buffer, cosine);
printf("e to %s = %f\n\n", buffer, etox);
exit(EXIT_SUCCESS);
}
```

8.3 Iteration statements

There are three types of interation statements, or loops, used in C. These are while statements, do-while statements and for statements and, as in most high level languages, these loops can be nested.

8.3.1 while

The simple while loop uses the following general form

```
while (conditional_expression)
   {
   /* statements */
   }
```

This construction is read as "while the conditional expression is true execute the statements within the braces, when the conditional expression is false ignore the statements within the braces and end the loop".

The conditional expression is evaluated before the loop starts and before every subsequent loop. This means that if the expression is false before the first loop then the statements within the braces are never executed. The loop does not have to have any executable statements within the braces and in this case the outline construction described above can be used to hold up a program until the conditional expression is false.

8.3.2 do-while

If the while statement is used to test a conditional expression at the foot of a loop then the reserved word do is used at the head of the loop to create a do-while loop. The do-while loop uses the following general form

```
do
   {
   /* statements */
   }
while (conditional_expression);
```

Unlike the while loop, which tests the conditional expression at the head of the loop, the statements within the braces of a do-while loop are always executed at least once before the test has the opportunity to end the loop. When the conditional expression is false then the loop ends. Notice that there is a semicolon after the conditional expression in the do-while loop but not after the conditional expression in the while loop.

The do-while loop is similar to the REPEAT-UNTIL loop used in BASIC except that the REPEAT-UNTIL loop is executed while the conditional expression is false and the do-while loop in C is executed while the conditional expression is true. For this reason REPEAT-UNTIL and do-while loops are said to be logically opposite.

The program arctan demonstrates the use of do-while loops as well as some complicated conditional expressions in the calculation of the inverse tangent. This calculation uses the following formulae

-1.0 < x < 1.0

$$arctan(x) = +or- \left(\frac{x^3}{3} - \frac{x^5}{5} + \frac{x^7}{7} - ... \right)$$

-1.0 >= x >= 1.0

$$arctan(x) = +or- \left(\frac{pi}{2} - \frac{1}{x} + \frac{1}{3x^3} - \frac{1}{5x^5} + \frac{1}{7x^7} - ... \right)$$

```c
/*
 * file name: arctan
 * calculate inverse tangent
 */

#include <stdio.h>
#include <stdlib.h>
#include <string.h>

#define PI_over_2 1.57079633
#define tiny 0.00000001
#define plenty 5000.0
#define absolute(x)  ((x)<0?(-x):(x))

int main(int argc, char *argv[])
  {
  double arctan, x, power, part, pass;
  double factor = 1.0;
  int test;
  char input[20];

  if (argc != 2)
    {
    printf("Enter x : ");
    gets(input);
    x = atof(input);
    }
  else
    {
    x = atof(argv[1]);
    strcpy(input, argv[1]);
    }
```

```
if (x < 0.0)
  {
  x = -x;
  factor = -factor;
  }
power = x;
if (x >= 1.0 || x <= -1.0)
  {
  arctan = PI_over_2;
  pass = 1.0;
  do
    {
    part = 1.0 / (pass * power);
    test = ((int) (pass + 1.0)) % 4;
    if (test == 0) arctan += part;
    else arctan -= part;
    power *= (x * x);
    pass += 2.0;
    }
  while (pass < plenty && absolute(part) > tiny);
  }
else
  {
  arctan = x;
  pass = 3.0;
  do
    {
    power *= (x * x);
    part = power / pass;
    test = ((int) (pass + 1.0)) % 4;
    if (test == 0) arctan -= part;
    else arctan += part;
    pass += 2.0;
    }
  while (pass < plenty && absolute(part) > tiny);
  }
arctan *= factor;
printf("arctan(%s) = %f radians\n", input, arctan);
exit(EXIT_SUCCESS);
}
```

8.3.3 for

The third type of iteration statement used in C is the for loop. This loop also has its BASIC counterpart in the FOR-NEXT loop available in every version of the BASIC language. The for loop in C uses quite a different general form to that used in BASIC and it is a more powerful programming tool than its BASIC counterpart.

The for loop uses the following general form

```
for (expression_1; conditional_expression; expression_2)
   {
   /* statements */
   }
```

Expression_1 is used to initialise a variable which controls the loop. It will commonly be something like x=1 or a=0 and so on. This expression is followed by a semicolon.

The conditional_expression is just like the conditional expression used in the while loop. It is evaluated at the beginning of the loop and the statements within the braces are only executed while the conditional expression is true. It will commonly be something like x < 10 or a <= 20 and so on. The conditional expression is also followed by a semicolon.

Expression_2 is evaluated at the end of each loop. This expression is often (but not necessarily) used to alter the control variable set up in expression_1. Any legal expression can be used. For example, x++ or a-- and so on. Because this expression is evaluated at the end of the loop it does not matter if, for example, x++ or ++x is used to increment a control variable. This is one occasion when x++ and ++x are equivalent. Expression_2 is not followed by a semicolon.

The for loop is demonstrated in the program sqroot which uses the Newton Raphson method to calculate the square root of a positive floating point number.

```
/*
 * file name: sqroot
 * calculate the square root of a number
 */

#include <stdio.h>
#include <stdlib.h>

int main(int argc, char *argv[])
   {
   double answer = 1.0;
```

```
double decimal;
register int loop;
char buffer[20];

if (argc != 2)
  {
  printf("Enter decimal number : ");
  gets(buffer);
  decimal = atof(buffer);
  }
else decimal = atof(argv[1]);
if (decimal < 0)
  {
  puts("Use a positive number");
  exit(EXIT_FAILURE);
  }
for (loop = 1; loop < 25; loop++)
  {
  answer = (answer + (decimal/answer)) / 2.0;
  }
printf("The square root of %g is %g\n", decimal,
   answer);
exit(EXIT_SUCCESS);
}
```

The for loop can be made to act exactly like the while loop by leaving out both expression_1 and expression_2. If you choose to use this construction then you must not leave out the semicolons which normally follow expression_1 and the conditional expression. The for loop equivalent of the while loop is

```
for (; conditional_expression; )
  {
  /* statements */
  }
```

8.3.4 break

The reserved word break can be used to end the looping in any interation statement. Using break within a loop is usually associated with a conditional expression as shown below

```
while (conditional_expression_1)
  {
  /* statements */

  if (conditional_expression_2)
    {
    /* statements */
    break; /* end the while loop */
    }

  /* statements */
  }
```

8.3.5 continue

The reserved word continue can also be used within any iteration statement to jump straight to the next pass in the loop. This can be used to avoid executing unnecessary or undesirable instructions and it is usually associated with a conditional expression.

```
while (conditional_expression_1)
  {
  /* statements */

  if (conditional_expression_2)
    {
    /* statements */
    continue; /* start next pass */
    }

  /* statements */
  }
```

In this case the next pass in the loop will start immediately after all the statements associated with conditional_expression_2 have been executed.

8.3.6 goto

The goto statement can also be used to produce loops by jumping to labels within a function. Jumping around in programs with goto cannot be recommended and the best thing to do with the goto statement is to ignore it.

Functions and Macros

9.1 Functions

A function in C has a wider meaning than that given to a function in mathematics or to a function in BASIC. A function in mathematics is something which has a value associated with its name and this, broadly speaking, is also true for a function in BASIC. A function in C incorporates both the BASIC and the mathematical ideas of a function, but C functions can also be used in much the same way that BASIC uses procedures and subroutines, although a function in C is much more like a subroutine in FORTRAN than a subroutine in BASIC. It is possible to mimic BASIC subroutines with C functions, but no experienced C programmer would want to mimic BASIC subroutines.

A function in C is a block of code which is created to deal with a particular task or group of related tasks. It is identified and called by a unique name and can accept parameters to receive information from other functions. A function can have a value associated with its name but, unlike a BASIC function, it doesn't have to have a value associated with its name. A function that does not have a value associated with its name is known as a void function. There are no local functions in C. All functions are global.

Every C program has a function called main. The function main always returns an integer value and so it is always declared as type int. The main function can call other functions and C programs use a hierarchy of functions with main at the root of a hierarchical tree of functions.

9.2 Function prototypes

The ANSI standard for C has adopted the use of function prototypes. A function prototype declares the type of the value returned by the function and the types of the parameters received by the function. The following outline code declares a function named funct which returns a value of type int and which passes three parameters of types char, int and double. The parameter identifiers are c, i and d respectively.

```
int main(void)
  {
  int funct(char c, int i, double d);

  /* statements */
  }
```

Specifying the return type and parameter types enables better error checking in ANSI C than in other dialects of the language. After a function has been declared it also has to be defined. For example

```
int main(void)
  {
  int funct(char c, int i, double d); /* declare */
  char cc = 'c'
  int ii = 1;
  double dd = 4.5;

  funct(cc, ii, dd); /* call the function */
  exit(EXIT_SUCCESS);
  }

int funct(char c, int i, double d) /* define */
  {
  /* statements */
  return i;
  }
```

The first line of a function definition is similar to the function declaration except that it is not terminated with a semicolon. The outline function definition shown above also declares the parameters c, i and d as local variables within the function funct. The function call

```
funct(cc, ii, dd);
```

passes the arguments cc, ii and dd to the function funct where the parameters c, i and d become the local variables c, i and d.

A function declaration can be made at the global level, usually between the include directives and main, or at a local level within a function. When a function is declared at a global level the declaration is valid throughout the file in which it is declared but a declaration made within a function is only valid in that function. Although a function definition is always global and a function can only be defined once it can be declared locally as many times as required. If a function is called from main and from a function funct then the same function can be declared locally in both main and funct but it can only be defined globally outside all the other functions.

If the function funct is defined before the function main then the function definition is also a function declaration and there is no need to use a function prototype in the function main. For example

```
   int funct(char c, int i, double d)  /* declare and define
*/
      {
      /* statements */
      return i;
      }

   int main(void)
      {
      char cc = 'c'
      int ii = 1;
      double dd = 4.5;

      funct(cc, ii, dd); /* call the function */
      exit(EXIT_SUCCESS);
      }
```

Programming style is a matter for the individual and some programmers prefer to define functions in this upside down order and save themselves the trouble of declaring function prototypes.

9.3 Passing arguments to main

When the function main accepts arguments typed after the application file name these arguments are passed to main and identified by two parameters typed after the function name. For example

```
   int main(int argc, char *argv[]);
      {
      /* statements */
      }
```

The parameters are an integer identified as the variable argc and an array of char pointers, argv. The variable argc stores the number of arguments typed after the application filename plus one, and each element in the array of pointers points to an argument. This technique is described in detail in chapter two and if you work through the many example programs in this book you will find that using arguments typed after the file name is one way of passing information to main. If arguments are not accepted after the application file name then main is defined as follows

```
int main(void)
  {
  /* statements */
  }
```

Any function which does not use parameters to accept values from its calling function should declare a void or empty parameter list in this way. If a function neither uses parameters nor returns a value then it is declared and defined as type void with a void parameter list.

9.4 The general form of functions

C function definitions use the following general form

```
type identifier(type arg_1, type arg_2, ..., type arg_n)
  {
  prototypes
  declarations
  statements
  return
  }
```

Every function has a type. If a function returns an integer then it is type int, if it returns a double precision floating point number then it is type double, if it does not return a value then it is type void, and so on. The function main always returns an integer and it is therefore always type int.

The function identifier can use up to 31 alpha-numeric characters including the underscore character. No other characters can be used and the first character must always be an alphabetic character or the underscore. In ANSI C all the characters of a function identifier are significant. It is the usual practice to use the underscore as the first character of a system function identifier and for this reason you should restrict the first character of any user-defined function identifier to the alphabetic characters from a to z and from A to Z.

The program product shows how arguments are passed from the function main and received as parameters by the function product_of. The program also shows how a value can be associated with the function product_of.

```
/*
 * file name: product
 * demonstrate passing arguments
 */

#include <stdio.h>
#include <stdlib.h>

int main(void)
   {
   int product_of(int m, int n);
   int i=2, j=3;
   int k;

   k = product_of(i, j);
   printf("%d * %d = %d\n", i, j, k);
   exit(EXIT_SUCCESS);
   }

int product_of(int m, int n)
   {
   return m * n;
   }
```

In this example the two integers i and j are passed to the function product_of which accepts them as the parameters m and n. The function returns the product of the two integers by using the return statement to associate the product with the function name. The function product_of is said to hand back a value to the main function using the return statement. The value handed back is assigned to the variable k.

The return statement will always associate the expression following the keyword return with the function identifier and immediately return to the calling function, even if return is deeply nested within loops in the called function. If the return statement is not used and the function definition simply ends with a closing brace then an unpredictable value will be associated with the function identifier.

The value handed back by a function must be of the same type as the variable to which it is assigned. In the above example the function product_of returns the value of an integer expression which is assigned to an integer k in the function main. You should not try to mix variable types by assigning, for example, a double precision floating point number to an integer.

The value handed back by a function can be used as an argument and passed to another function, but you can only use a function as a argument in this way if the function uses the return statement to associate a value with the function identifier.

9.5 Passing addresses to functions

Addresses can be passed to functions as arguments to allow a function to manipulate the contents of those addresses. Using this technique effectively allows a function to hand back more than one value to the calling function. You can use the & operator to pass the address of a variable to a function and the receiving function then uses the * operator to manipulate the data stored at that address. The return statement is optional when addresses are passed and used in this way and the called function can be declared as a void function, although this is not absolutely essential.

```
/*
 * file name: increase
 * demonstrate passing addresses to a function
 */

#include <stdio.h>
#include <stdlib.h>

int main(void)
  {
  void increment(int *m, int *n);
  int i=2, j=3;

  increment(&i, &j); /* pass the addresses of i and j */
  printf("2 + 2 = %d 3 + 2 = %d\n", i, j);
  exit(EXIT_SUCCESS);
  }

void increment(int *m, int *n)
  {
  *m += 2;
  *n += 2;
  }
```

In the program increase the addresses of the local variables i and j in main are passed to the function increment where these addresses are assigned to the pointers m and n. The expression *m in the function increment is read as "the data stored in address m" and the statement

```
*m += 2;
```

is read as "add two to the data stored in address m". It should be clear that the increment and assign statements in the function increment are altering the values assigned to the local variables i and j in main.

9.6 Recursive functions

Functions can be defined in terms of themselves. A function defined in this way is said to be recursive. The factorial of a number can be calculated recursively and this is demonstrated in the program factorial. An interesting point to note about the program factorial is that there are two local variables called decimal, one in main and one in the function factorial. Although these variable have the same name they are completely independent of one another. They are local variables and only available in the function within which they are declared. The program uses double precision floating point variables to calculate the factorials of integer numbers because the factorials of even quite small numbers are outside the range of integers.

```
/*
 * file name: factorial
 * calculate the factorial of a number
 */

#include <stdio.h>
#include <stdlib.h>

int main(int argc, char *argv[])
  {
  double factorial(double decimal);
  double decimal, answer;
  char buffer[20];

  if (argc != 2)
    {
    printf("Enter integer : ");
    gets(buffer);
    decimal = atof(buffer);
    }
  else decimal = atof(argv[1]);
  answer = factorial(decimal);
  printf("%2.0f factorial = %-g\n", decimal, answer);
  exit(EXIT_SUCCESS);
  }
```

```
double factorial(double decimal)
  {
  if (decimal <= 1.0) return 1.0;
  else return decimal * factorial(decimal - 1.0);
  }
```

Compile the program and type, for example

```
factorial 10
```

or

```
factorial 15
```

The program will respond by printing the factorial of the argument.

When the function factorial is called with an argument greater than 1.0 the function calls a copy of itself with the argument reduced by one. This procedure continues until factorial is called with an argument of 1.0, which is the terminating condition for the recursive calls. All recursive functions must have a terminating condition otherwise the function gets locked into an endless loop of calling copies of itself.

There are a number of informal rules which will help to keep recursive functions out of trouble. These include

Rule 1

Do not write statements in a recursive function after the recursive call.

Rule 2

Minimize the complexity of all recursive functions.

Rule 3

Only use recursion if it improves the efficiency of a program. If there is an alternative method which is just as efficient as recursion then use the alternative method.

9.7 Variable length argument lists

The function printf is always used with at least one argument, a control string, which performs a number of tasks. The control string is used to display text, to indicate the conversion specification of the list of arguments which follows the control string and, most importantly, to use the number of conversion specifiers in the control string to indicate how many arguments follow the string.

All functions which use variable length argument lists need to pass an argument which specifies the otherwise unknown number of arguments. By convention this argument is known as parmN in user-defined functions and it is the last named argument in the list of arguments. The argument parmN is used to pass an integer value which specifies the number of arguments to follow. The use of the parameter parmN can be demonstrated in a function which sums a list of arguments. The first argument passed to this function is the only named parameter, parmN, and this will be used to specify the number of arguments to follow. For example, the function call

```
add(2, 1.2, 2.3);
```

will be used to add the two arguments 1.2 and 2.3 and return their sum.

The function prototype and the function definition have to be declared with parmN as the last named parameter. parmN is followed by ... to represent the unknown list of arguments.

In the following outline program there is only one named parameter, parmN. We can precede parmN with any number of other named parameters but remember that parmN has to be the last named parameter.

```
#include <stdarg.h>

int main(void)
  {
  double add(int parmN, ...);

  /* statements */
  }

double add(int parmN, ...)
  {
  /* statements */
  }
```

The header file stdarg.h declares a data type and defines three macros for advancing through a list of arguments whose number and types are not known to the called function when it is translated. We need to include this file when we define our own functions with variable length argument lists but stdarg.h is not required for functions such as printf and scanf.

The data type va_list is used to declare a pointer to the list of arguments. By convention, this pointer is called ap and the pointer ap is declared as type va_list in the called function as follows

```
double add(int parmN, ...)
  {
  va_list ap;
  va_start(ap, parmN);

  /* ap points to first argument after parmN */
  }
```

The macro va_start is used to initialise the pointer ap. This macro takes two arguments, the pointer ap and the number of parameters, parmN. After initialisation with va_start the pointer ap points to the first argument following parmN.

After the pointer ap has been initialised with the macro va_start the macro va_arg can be used to return the argument and to advance the pointer ap to point to the next argument. The macro va_arg takes two arguments, the pointer ap and the data type of the argument to be returned. The data type of each argument must be made available to va_arg. There can be no implicit casting of values. It is easier to implement functions with only one data type for the variable length list of arguments but, if it is necessary to mix data types, information about the data types must also be passed to the function.

```
double add(int parmN, ...)
  {
  double value;
  va_list ap;
  va_start(ap, parmN);

  value = va_arg(ap, double);
/*
 * va_arg returns the value of the argument
 * after parmN, ap points to the next argument
 */
  va_end(ap);
  return;
  }
```

The last macro to be used is va_end which has to be used after the last call to va_arg. The macro va_end takes the pointer ap as an argument and va_end must be used to facilitate an ordered return from the called function.

The use of variable length argument lists is demonstrated in the program addition.

```
/*
 * file name: addition
 * demonstrate variable length argument lists
 */

#include <stdio.h>
#include <stdlib.h>
#include <stdarg.h>

int main(void)
   {
   double add(int parmN, ...);
   double total;

   total = add(3, 1.2, 2.3, 3.4);
   printf("\n1.2 + 2.3 + 3.4 = %3.1f\n\n", total);
   total = add(2, 1.2, 2.3);
   printf("\n1.2 + 2.3 = %3.1f\n", total);
   exit(EXIT_SUCCESS);
   }
double add(int parmN, ...)
   {
   va_list ap;
   double value;
   double sum = 0.0;

   va_start(ap, parmN);
   while (parmN--)
      {
      value = va_arg(ap, double);
      printf("next argument = %3.1f\n", value);
      sum += value;
      }
   va_end(ap);
   return sum;
   }
```

9.8 Macros

In C, both the procedures and functions familiar to BASIC programmers can be translated into either C functions or macros. Complex procedures and functions are usually translated into functions but simple BASIC procedures and functions can also be translated into C macros. Macros in C are program code substitutions defined using the preprocessor #define directive. Preprocessor directives and the rules for creating macros are discussed in chapter three.

Choosing whether to use functions or macros in C is not quite as simple as recognizing the difference between complex and simple procedures. If speed of execution is important then macros always execute faster than functions. When a function is called the values or addresses associated with the arguments have to be passed to the function and values have to be returned. All this takes time. Macros, on the other hand, are program code substitutions which don't have to be called and which execute without the delays associated with calling and returning from functions. Because macros are program code substitutions they don't have to be type specific and it is possible to use the same macro with different data types.

Although macros are faster than functions, using functions rather than macros can reduce the size of a program. Every time a macro is used in a program the entire code of the macro is substituted for the macro name and the program gets bigger every time a macro is used. Macros are best used for short routines when the increase in program size will be minimised.

Long macros are difficult to read and understand and you must not use recursion in macro definitions. Macros have to be defined on one line and you cannot pass pointers to macros as arguments.

9.9 Types of macros

There are three basic types of macros: definition macros, function macros and expression macros. The program macrotypes illustrates all three basic types and it should be quite clear from this example why definition and expression macros are thus described. A definition macro substitutes a character string for a symbolic constant and an expression macro substitutes an expression for the macro identifier.

Function macros are macros which emulate more complex functions and they are used extensively in C. The macro gets is defined in stdio.h using the more complex function fgets and many more function macros are defined in the standard ANSI library. It is worth remembering that function macros are not true functions, they are code substitutions made during compilation, although we often use function macros as if they are functions without knowing that they are in fact macros.

```
/*
 * file name: macrotypes
 * illustrate the different types of macros
 */

#include <stdio.h>
```

```
#include <stdlib.h>

/* definition macro */
#define CARDINAL 10

/* expression macro */
#define square(x)  ((x)*(x))

/* function macro */
#define answer(x,y) printf("\n%d squared = %d\n",x,y)

int main(void)
   {
   int a, b;

   a = CARDINAL;
   b = square(a);
   answer(a, b);
   exit(EXIT_SUCCESS);
   }
```

10

Pointers and addresses

10.1 Pointers

Pointers are used extensively in C. A pointer is a special type of integer variable which is used to store an address. This can be the address of another variable, the address of an array or even the address of a function.

Pointers are associated with the two reserved words, * and &. The reserved word * has two meanings when associated with pointers as well as its other quite independent use as the multiplication symbol. Variables are declared as pointers by using * immediately before the pointer identifier. It is possible to declare pointers to any type of object and to declare void pointers, which are also known as generic pointers. The following code demonstrates how the reserved word * is used to declare pointers.

```
int main(void)
  {
  char letter, *c_point;
  int cardinal, *i_point;
  double real, *d_point;
  void *v_point;

  /* statements */
  }
```

The first of these declarations declares a character variable, letter, and a pointer to a character variable, c_point. At this stage the variable letter is not associated with the pointer c_point in any way other than that they are both variables of type char. In order to associate a pointer with a variable it is necessary to use the reserved word &, which means "the address of". This is demonstrated in the program point.

```
/*
 * file name: point
 * demonstrate the use of pointers
 */

#include <stdio.h>
#include <stdlib.h>

int main(void)
  {
  int cardinal = 0;
  int *i_point;

  i_point = &cardinal;
  *i_point = 128;
  puts("cardinal should = 128");
  printf("cardinal = %d\n", cardinal);
  exit(EXIT_SUCCESS);
  }
```

The program point declares and initialises an integer variable, cardinal, and declares an integer pointer, i_point, with the following code

```
int cardinal = 0;
int *i_point;
```

The pointer in the second declaration must never be initialised in the same way as the variable in the first declaration. The integer pointer i_point is given a meaningful value in the next line of code where it is associated with the variable cardinal by assigning the address of cardinal to the pointer i_point.

```
i_point = &cardinal;
```

This assignment makes i_point a pointer to the variable cardinal. The only way to initialise a pointer is to assign an address to the pointer. The statement above uses the reserved word & to assign the address of the variable cardinal to the pointer i_point. The next statement in the program point is

```
*i_point = 128;
```

and this instructs the computer to store the value 128 in the address pointed to by the pointer i_point. This statement is equivalent to

```
cardinal = 128;
```

because the address of the integer variable cardinal is the address stored in the pointer i_point. Always remember that we cannot do anything meaningful with a pointer until it has been assigned an address. Using a pointer which has not been assigned an address can be compared to posting a letter without an address, it's possible but it's not a good idea.

It has already been explained that the reserved word * has two uses with pointers. The first use is to declare a variable as a pointer with a declaration such as

```
int *i_point;
```

and the second use is illustrated in the line of code in the program point which reads

```
*i_point = 128;
```

which is read as "store 128 in the address pointed to by i_point".

Because * has two meanings it is logically incorrect and potentially very dangerous to initialise a pointer with the following code, which confuses the two meanings of * in one statement.

```
int *i_point = 0;
```

This code is read as "declare a pointer to an integer variable and call the pointer i_point, then store zero in the address stored in i_point."

At first sight this seems to be quite in order but it is important to realise that declaring a variable in this way does not initialise the variable. The pointer, i_point, will have an unpredictable value when it is declared and the address stored in i_point could be anything. Storing a number in the unpredictable address pointed to by i_point is a risky business which could cause all sorts of problems. The golden rule with pointers is never do anything with a pointer until it has been assigned a meaningful address.

The BASIC indirection operators PEEK and POKE are similar to pointers but the use of pointers in C is far more important than peeking and poking is in BASIC. Pointers are used in C to pass arrays, structures and even the addresses of functions to functions, to receive multiple results back from functions, and when using strings and linked lists. Pointers must be used with the standard input/output scan-formatted function, scanf, which simply will not work properly without pointers. It is vital to understand the use of pointers and to remember the meanings of & and *.

&variable_name   means "the address of the variable called variable_name"

*pointer_name   means "the contents of the address stored in the
                       pointer called pointer_name"
double *pointer_name means "declare a pointer called pointer_name as
                       a pointer to type double"

10.2 Pointers and character strings

Pointers can be used to point to permanently stored text within a program. A pointer
used to point to a character string created during compilation can have either a static
or an automatic storage class. Which ever storage class is chosen for the pointer will
depend on the context in which the pointer is being used but the character string to
which it points should be regarded as a permanent, read only char array and no
attempt should be made to alter the character string during program execution. Using
pointers in this way is demonstrated in the program pointmsg.

```
/*
 * file name: pointmsg
 * using pointers to a character string
 */

#include <stdio.h>
#include <stdlib.h>

int main(void)
  {
  static char *point_msg = "Hello, how are you?";
  static char text[] = "and now for something else";

  printf("message = %s\n", point_msg);
  point_msg = text;
  printf("pointing to new text: %s\n", point_msg);
  exit(EXIT_SUCCESS);
  }
```

In this example the compiler stores the first message as a char array with 20 elements
(19 characters and a null end-of-text marker byte) and the address of the char array is
assigned to the pointer point_msg. The pointer is a variable which can be modified
during the execution of the program but the character string to which it points is a
constant that cannot be altered. After displaying the first message the address stored
in the pointer is altered to point to the second array. This does not have any effect on
the characters of the first message which are read only and completely uneffected by
this assignment.

10.3 Pointers and the cast operator

The cast operator can be used to cast a pointer of one type into a pointer of another type. If it is necessary, for example, to compare the address of char variable to the address of a variable of type int then the address of the char variable has to be cast into the type pointer to int. This does not cast the variable into type int, only the address. Notice that there is a difference between the cast operator for int, which is (int), and the cast operator pointer to int, which is (int *).

```
int main(void)
  {
  char letter;
  int *i_point;

  i_point = (int *) &letter;

  /* statements */
  }
```

10.4 Pointers and scanf

Either pointers to variables or the addresses of variables are used by the input function scanf. When we use scanf to read the keyboard and store information read from the keyboard in a variable then we can use the reserved word & with variable identifiers to ensure that the arguments passed to scanf are addresses. As an alternative we can use pointers which have been assigned the addresses of the required variables. It amounts to the same thing.

For example, the program scanf can be used to read an integer into the variable cardinal, but notice that the function scanf uses &cardinal to pass the address of cardinal to scanf. It does not pass the variable identifier, it passes the address of the variable.

```
/*
 * file name: scanf
 * using pointers with scanf
 */

#include <stdio.h>
#include <stdlib.h>

int main(void)
  {
```

```
int cardinal;

puts("Enter an integer number");
scanf("%d", &cardinal);
/*
 * &cardinal means "the address of cardinal"
 * using the address of cardinal is equivalent
 * to using a pointer to cardinal
 */
printf("cardinal = %d\n", cardinal);
exit(EXIT_SUCCESS);
}
```

There is much more to the function scanf than this simple example illustrates but we can only use pointers to variables or addresses with scanf. This function is examined in much more detail in chapter six.

10.5 Functions that alter variables via parameters

Pointers can be used to pass the addresses of a number of variables to a function. The receiving function can then use the reserved word * to manipulate the data stored in those addresses. In this way the data stored in the original variables can be accessed within the called function and a function can effectively hand back more than one value.

The program handback demonstrates how pointers can be used to alter a number of variables and effectively hand back those altered variables to the calling function. In this case the addresses of the variables sine, cosine and etox are all passed to the function calculate where the values stored in these variables are manipulated. The new values of the variables are handed back to the function main when calculate executes the return statement.

```
/*
 * file name: handback
 * calculate trig functions from first principles
 * and demonstrate pointers
 */

#include <stdio.h>
#include <stdlib.h>

int main(void)
```

```
  {
  void calculate(double *sine, double *cosine,
                 double *etox, double x);
  double sine, cosine, etox, x;
  char buffer[20];

  printf("Enter x (radians): ");
  x = atof(fgets(buffer, 19, stdin));
  calculate(&sine, &cosine, &etox, x);
  printf("sin(x) = %f\n", sine);
  printf("cos(x) = %f\n", cosine);
  printf("e to x = %f\n\n", etox);
  exit(EXIT_SUCCESS);
  }

void calculate(double *sine, double *cosine,
               double *etox, double x)
  {
  double power, part;
  double factorial = 1.0;
  register int loop;

  *sine = x;
  *cosine = 1.0;
  power = x;
  *etox = 1.0 + x;
  for (loop = 2; loop <= 30; loop++)
     {
     factorial *= (double) loop;
     power *= x;
     part = power / factorial;
     *etox += part;
     switch (loop % 4)
       {
       case 0:
         {
         *cosine += part;
         break;
         }
       case 1:
         {
         *sine += part;
         break;
         }
```

```
        case 2:
          {
          *cosine -= part;
          break;
          }
        case 3:
          {
          *sine -= part;
          break;
          }
        default:
          {
          puts("Error !!!");
          exit(EXIT_FAILURE);
          }
        }
      }
   return;
   }
```

The program handback uses the function fgets to get a character string from the keyboard. This use of fgets is equivalent to the BASIC command INPUT and it is examined along with quite a number of other i/o functions in chapter six.

10.6 Pointers and arrays

An integer array can be declared with the following code

```
int ordinal[10];
```

In this case an integer array is created with 10 elements, indexed as elements 0 to 9. The zeroth element is written as ordinal[0], the first element as ordinal[1] and so on up to the ninth element with ordinal[9]. When the array is created the compiler uses the identifier of the array as a pointer constant for the array and stores the starting address of the array in that pointer constant. In this case the pointer constant ordinal is a pointer to the zeroth element of the array ordinal[10]. It is important to notice that this pointer to the array is a constant and not a variable.

When an array is declared the array identifier becomes a pointer to the array and every indexed reference to the array can be replaced with an equivalent pointer with an offset. The pointer *ordinal is equivalent to ordinal[0], the pointer *(ordinal + 1), which includes the offset 1, is equivalent to ordinal[1] and so on up to *(ordinal + 9) which is equivalent to ordinal[9]. Integer arrays usually use four bytes per element but it is not necessary include scaling with the offset. The compiler takes care of scaling by multiplying the offset by the number of bytes per element. In every respect the array identifier is a pointer to the array but remember that the address stored in that pointer is a constant and must not be altered.

When an array is passed to a function it is only necessary to pass the address of the array and not the complete array. Functions do not need to copy the original array into local storage, which can take time and space with large arrays. Instead the array identifier can be passed as a pointer and the called function can use the memory reserved for the original array.

The program array demonstrates how an array identifier is passed to a function and how the contents of the array can be manipulated from within the called function.

```c
/*
 * file name: array
 * an array identifier is passed to a function as a pointer
 */

#include <stdio.h>
#include <stdlib.h>

int main(void)
   {
   void values(int list[]);
   int list[5];
   values(list);
   puts("list[2] should = 128");
   puts("list[3] should = 255");
   printf("\nlist[2] = %d\n", list[2]);
   printf("list[3] = %d\n", *(list + 3));
   exit(EXIT_SUCCESS);
   }

void values(int list[])
   {
   int *point;

   point = &list[2]; /* point to list[2] */
   *point = 128; /* equivalent to list[2] = 128 */
   list[3] = 255; /* same effect but much easier! */
   return;
   }
```

10.7 Pointer arithmetic

Pointer variables always contain addresses and it is possible to perform a limited range of arithmetic operations on these addresses to obtain new addresses. Performing arithmetic operations on pointer variables is quite different from performing arithmetic operations on other types of variables. When an integer is added to or subtracted from the address stored in a pointer the compiler scales the result so that the pointer always points to an appropriate address.

If an integer, i, is added to a pointer, p, then the sum is evaluated as if by the expression

```
(int) p + (i * (int) sizeof(type_pointed_to))
```

and if a pointer, p, is subtracted from another pointer, q, then the difference is evaluated as if by the expression

```
((int) q - (int) p) / (int) sizeof(type_pointed_to)
```

To clarify what these expressions mean consider a pointer, p, to an integer array. In this case an array could have been declared as

```
int p[20];
```

The pointer p points to the zeroth element of the array p[20]. This means that

```
*p
```

and

```
p[0]
```

are equivalent and, in general,

```
*(p+i)
```

and

```
p[i]
```

are equivalent.

This means that when an integer i is added to address stored in the pointer p the result is produced by adding the number of bytes required to store i integers to the address, so that the addresses p and p+i are i integers apart and not i bytes apart.

It is only possible to perform three arithmetic operations on pointer variables. These operations are integer addition, integer subtraction and the subtraction of addresses. No other operations are allowed. The result of an arithmetic operation on the address stored in a pointer will always be appropriately scaled for the pointer type. This means that we cannot mix pointer types in arithmetic expressions but, because we will probably never have any reason for doing so, this should not be a problem.

10.8 Pointers to functions

The start address of a function can be assigned to a pointer. In order to do this we must first declare a prototype of the function itself and then, after all the function prototypes and before the declaration of variables, a prototype of the pointer to the function. In the program funpoint the prototype of a function increment and the prototype of a pointer to the function increment are declared with the following code.

```
int increment(int cardinal); /* function prototype */
int (*fun_point)(int cardinal); /* pointer to function */
```

After prototyping, the identifier of an appropriate function can be assigned to the pointer. The function identifier is a pointer to the function in just the same way that an array identifier is a pointer to an array. A pointer to a function is a variable and the address of any appropriate function can be assigned to the pointer. This is demonstrated in the program funpoint.

```
/*
 * file name: funpoint
 * demonstrate pointers to functions
 */

#include <stdio.h>
#include <stdlib.h>

int main(void)
  {
  int increment(int cardinal);
  int decrement(int cardinal);
  int middleman(int (*fun_point)(int cardinal), int
    ordinal);
  int (*fun_point)(int cardinal);
  int cardinal = 1;
  fun_point = increment;
  cardinal = fun_point(cardinal);
  printf("1 + 1 = %d\n", cardinal);
```

```
    /* fun_point(cardinal) and increment(cardinal) are
       equivalent */
    fun_point = decrement;
    cardinal = fun_point(cardinal);
    printf("2 - 1 = %d\n", cardinal);
    /* fun_point(cardinal) and decrement(cardinal) are
       equivalent */
    cardinal = middleman(increment, cardinal);
    printf("1 + 1 = %d\n", cardinal);
    cardinal = middleman(decrement, cardinal);
    printf("2 - 1 = %d\n", cardinal);
    exit(EXIT_SUCCESS);
    }

int increment(int cardinal)
    {
    return ++cardinal;
    }

int decrement(int cardinal)
    {
    return --cardinal;
    }

int middleman(int (*fun_point)(int cardinal), int ordinal)
    {
    return fun_point(ordinal);
    }
```

In the program above the address of the function increment is assigned to the pointer fun_point and then the function increment is called from main by using

```
    fun_point = increment;
    cardinal = fun_point(cardinal);
    printf("1 + 1 = %d\n", cardinal);
```

these statements are equivalent to

```
    cardinal = increment(cardinal);
    printf("1 + 1 = %d\n", cardinal);
```

After the first function call using fun_point, the pointer fun_point is assigned the address of the function decrement and then the function decrement is called from main by using

```
fun_point = decrement;
cardinal = fun_point(cardinal);
printf("2 - 1 = %d\n", cardinal);
```

these statements are equivalent to

```
cardinal = increment(cardinal);
printf("1 + 1 = %d\n", cardinal);
```

By using pointers in this way two different functions of the same function type and with the same number and type of arguments can be called with one pointer related function call. A pointer to a function can also be passed to another function as an argument, just like any other pointer. This is demonstrated in the following statements taken from the program 'funpoint'.

```
cardinal = middleman(increment, cardinal);
printf("1 + 1 = %d\n", cardinal);

cardinal = middleman(decrement, cardinal);
printf("2 - 1 = %d\n", cardinal);
```

The function identifiers increment and decrement are passed to the function middleman as a pointer. The function middleman uses a pointer to a function to call the chosen function and returns either an incremented or a decremented integer cardinal. This technique will reduce the amount of coding needed if it ever becomes necessary to use pointers to functions to call functions.

10.9 Void pointers

Pointers declared as type void are a special and very useful type of pointer.

A pointer of type char can only be used to point to an object of type char and a pointer of type double can only be compared to another pointer of type double, and so on, but a pointer of type void can be used to point to any type of object and can be compared to a pointer of any type. Void pointers are known as generic pointers because they are not type specific like all other pointers.

A number of standard library functions, such as malloc, calloc and realloc, return void pointers. Because the values returned by these functions are generic pointers they can be assigned to any type of pointer without using the cast operator. Normally we can only assign returned pointers to pointers of the same type but we can assign pointers of type void to any type of pointer and compare pointers of type void to pointers of any other type in logical expressions without generating an error.

The only thing that cannot be done with void pointers is to use pointer arithmetic. The reason for this is that the generality of the pointer makes it impossible for the compiler to work out the scaling of the offsets to be added to or subtracted from the pointer.

11

Arrays

11.1 Simple one dimensional arrays

C makes use of the concept of arrays in much the same way as most other high level languages but it is necessary to exercise more care when using arrays in C than in the other high level languages. C performs very few checks on the use of arrays and it is quite unforgiving to the programmer who fails to design his or her programs carefully.

Arrays are reserved areas of memory which can be addressed using one or more indices. The most simple array is a one dimensional array which can be compared to a list of items all of the same data type. A one dimensional, five element, double precision floating point array is declared in the following statement.

```
double list[5];
```

This statement will reserve enough memory to store five double precision numbers in adjacent, or contiguous, memory locations. The number of elements in an array is often referred to as the dimension of the array. This can be a little confusing if it is muddled up with the dimensionality of the array. The above example is definitely a one dimensional array, the dimension 5 is used to declare the size of the one dimensional array. Do not attempt to dimension arrays with zero or negative numbers of elements.

The dimension used to specify the size of an array must be a constant expression which evaluates to an integer or unsigned integer. You can not use a variable to dimension an array but you can use symbolic constants. If the symbolic constant SIZE is defined as

```
#define SIZE 5
```

then a one dimensional, 5 element array can be declared with

```
double list[SIZE];
```

The number in square brackets is the index or subscript of the array and, in the examples above, the index ranges from 0 to 4 (not from 1 to 5). The index of an array must have the type int or unsigned int whatever the type of the array element.

The element list[0] is read as "list subscript 0" or "list index 0" and, although this is the first element of the array, it is more convenient to refer to the first element as the zeroth element. It is important to get used to the idea of the elements of an array ranging from zero to one less than the size specified in the declaration of the array and to refer to the first element as the zeroth element might help to jog the memory. If you forget and start numbering the elements from 1 to the size of the array then the compiler will not report an error. But be warned, sooner rather than later a program will run into trouble if an attempt is made to access an element outside the reserved area of memory.

Every element in an array is of the same type. In the above example the type is double precision floating point. An array is not initialised by declaring it. This means that when an array is declared it will also need to be initialised if it is to contain known values.

11.2 Initialising arrays

Although it is not always necessary to initialise an array after declaring the array, it is necessary if the array is to contain known values. There are a number of ways of initialising an array and the method chosen usually depends on the size and storage class of the array. A simple two element array is declared and initialised in the program onedim.

```
/*
 * file name: onedim
 * declare and initialise an array
 */

#include <stdio.h>
#include <stdlib.h>

int main(void)
  {
  int list[2];

  list[0] = 0;
```

```
  list[1] = 1;
  printf("list[0] = %d\n", list[0]);
  printf("list[1] = %d\n", list[1]);
  exit(EXIT_SUCCESS);
  }
```

An alternative method for initialising relatively small arrays is to use the assignment operator and a block of data enclosed by braces. You can only initialise static local arrays or global arrays using this method.

```
/*
 * file name: small
 * declare and initialise an array
 */

#include <stdio.h>
#include <stdlib.h>

int main(void)
  {
  static int list[2] = {0,1};

  printf("list[0] = %d\n", list[0]);
  printf("list[1] = %d\n", list[1]);
  exit(EXIT_SUCCESS);
  }
```

This method cannot be used with automatic arrays, only with static arrays and external arrays. External arrays are static by default and in general this method can only be used with static arrays. The compiler will report an error if you try to use this method with any other storage class. You should note that the semicolon after the closing brace of the data is an essential part of the syntax.

Yet another alternative, which is often used with large arrays, is to initialise the array with a for loop. A 10 element array is declared and then initialised with a suitable for loop in the program large. When this method is used to initialise an array then it is important to ensure that any expression within the square brackets following an array identifier evaluates to an integer, and preferably an unsigned integer.

```
/*
 * file name: large
 * declare and initialise an array
 */
```

```
#include <stdio.h>
#include <stdlib.h>

int main(void)
  {
  double list[10];
  register unsigned int index;
  for (index = 0; index < 10; index++)
    {
    list[index] = (double) index;
    }
  for (index = 0; index < 10; index++)
    {
    printf("list[%d] = %f\n", index, list[index]);
    }
  exit(EXIT_SUCCESS);
  }
```

11.3 The input of data into arrays

The individual elements in an array can be assigned values interactively using any of the standard input functions. The program input uses the functions fgets and scanf to read the keyboard and the values read are assigned to the elements list[0], list[1] and list[2].

```
/*
 * file name: input
 * read into an array element
 */

#include <stdio.h>
#include <stdlib.h>

int main(void)
  {
  float list[3];
  char buffer[20];

  printf("Enter a floating point number : ");
  fgets(buffer, 19, stdin);
  list[0] = (float) atof(buffer);
  printf("and another : ");
  scanf("%f", &list[1]);
```

```
printf("and another : ");
scanf("%f", (list + 2));
printf("list[0] = %f\n", list[0]);
printf("list[1] = %f\n", list[1]);
printf("list[2] = %f\n", list[2]);
exit(EXIT_SUCCESS);
}
```

The function scanf only accepts pointers to data items in its list of arguments after the control string. The argument &list[1] is read as "the address of the element list[1]". The identifier of an array is a pointer to the first byte of the memory reserved for the array and the expression (list + 2) uses pointer arithmetic to evaluate the address of list[2]. Both these arguments are pointers to the addresses of their respective elements in the array list.

11.4 Multi-dimensional arrays

Multi-dimensional arrays are available in C and, in practice, the size and dimensionality is usually only limited by the amount of memory available. A two dimensional 5 by 5 array can be declared with, For example

```
double table[5] [5];
```

A three dimensional array with, For example

```
double cube[5] [5] [5];
```

Ex-BASIC and ex-Pascal programmers should be particularly careful not to use the following incorrect syntax when declaring a two dimensional array.

```
double table[5,5]; /* not the same as double table[5]
[5]; */
```

This is not an illegal declaration in C, it is just confusing a comma expression with the declaration of an array. The comma expression 5,5 evaluates to 5 and the above declaration reserves enough memory for a one dimensional array with 5 elements. It will not reserve the correct amount of memory for the required array and it is quite simply the wrong way to declare a two dimensional array even though it doesn't generate a compilation error.

A two dimensional array can be declared and then initialised using nested for loops as shown in the program multi.

```
/*
 * file name: multi
 * declare and initialise a multi-dimensional array
 */

#include <stdio.h>
#include <stdlib.h>

#define ROW_SIZE 5
#define COLUMN_SIZE 2

int main(void)
  {
  int table[ROW_SIZE] [COLUMN_SIZE];
  register int row, column;

  for (row = 0; row < ROW_SIZE; row++)
    {
    for (column = 0; column < COLUMN_SIZE; column++)
      {
      table[row] [column] = (row * 10) + column ;
      }
    }
  for (row = 0; row < ROW_SIZE; row++)
    {
    for (column = 0; column < COLUMN_SIZE; column++)
      {
      printf("table[%d] [%d] = %02d, ",
      row, column, table[row] [column]);
      }
    printf("\n");
    }
  exit(EXIT_SUCCESS);
  }
```

Multi-dimensional arrays can also be initialised by assigning a block of data to the array, as described earlier for one dimensional arrays. This technique, demonstrated in the program assign, is only suitable for relatively small multi-dimensional static arrays. The extra braces in the statement

```
static int table[2] [2] = {{0,1},
                           {2,3}};
```

are used to emphasize the two dimensional properties of the array. They are not an essential part of the syntax and the following statement is entirely equivalent.

```
static int table[2] [2] = {0,1,2,3};
```

In both cases the value 0 is assigned to table[0] [0], 1 is assigned to table[0] [1], 2 is assigned to table[1] [0], and 3 is assigned to table[1] [1].

When a two dimensional array is used to create a table, the left hand index usually represents the rows of the table and the right hand index usually represents the columns. The program assign demonstrates that the values in the data block are assigned a row at a time. This is an example of the general rule that when a data block is assigned to a multi-dimensional array then the rightmost index of the array changes fastest followed by the index to its immediate left, and so on until all the values in the data block are assigned to the array.

```
/*
 * file name: assign
 * declare and initialise a multi-dimensional array
 */

#include <stdio.h>
#include <stdlib.h>

#define ROW_SIZE 2
#define COLUMN_SIZE 2

int main(void)
  {
  static int table[ROW_SIZE] [COLUMN_SIZE] = {{0,1},
                                              {2,3}};
  puts("array initialised with");
  printf("static int table[2] [2] = {0,1,2,3};\n\n");
  printf("table[0] [0] = %d\n", table[0] [0]);
  printf("table[0] [1] = %d\n", table[0] [1]);
  printf("table[1] [0] = %d\n", table[1] [0]);
  printf("table[1] [1] = %d\n", table[1] [1]);
  exit(EXIT_SUCCESS);
  }
```

The declaration of an array determines how much memory is set aside for the data it is to contain. An unfortunate aspect of C is that it does not prevent a careless programmer using array indices outside the reserved area of memory. A common mistake is to assume that the elements of an array are numbered from one to the size of the array rather than from zero to one less than the size. This means that you must not try to use the index 5 on a five element array because index 5 refers to an area of memory which is outside the memory reserved for a 5 element array. C does not perform any bounds check and will not prevent you trying to access non-existent elements. The consequences of accessing non-existent elements are unpredictable and may or may not result in program crashes. Even if the program does not crash the effects will be unpredictable.

11.5 Arrays and functions

When an array identifier is passed to a function as an argument the function does not copy the original array into local storage. Instead the program passes a pointer to the array so that the function can use the memory reserved for the original array. The identifier of an array is a pointer to the first byte of memory reserved for the array and the array identifier is passed to a function rather than the array itself. The program appoint illustrates that the same area of memory is used for the array list in both main and in the function values.

```
/*
 * file name: appoint
 * an array identifier is passed to a function as a pointer
 */

#include <stdio.h>
#include <stdlib.h>

int main(void)
   {
   void values(int list[]);
   int list[5];

   printf("In main address of list[5] = %p\n", list);
   values (list);
   puts("list[3] should = 255");
   printf("list[3] = %d\n", list[3]);
   exit(EXIT_SUCCESS);
   }

void values(int list[])
   {
   printf("In values address of list[5] = %p\n", list);
   list[3] = 255;
   return;
```

```
   }
```

The program appoint declares an array list[5] but the prototype for the function values
does not include the size of the array. The definition of the function values does not
include the size of the array list either. It's a good idea to leave out the size of a one
dimensional array in the prototype and definition of a function in this way. It makes
the function more general and portable to other programs.

When one dimensional arrays are passed to functions there is no need to specify the
size of the array but when multi-dimensional arrays are passed it is essential to
specify the size of all but the leftmost dimension in both the prototype and the
definition of the function. The more general techniques for using pointers to pass
arrays to functions are illustrated in the program list.

```
/*
 * file name: list
 * pass arrays to functions
 */

#include <stdio.h>
#include <stdlib.h>

int main(void)
  {
  void function1(int list[]);
  void function2(int *list);
  void function3(int table[] [2]);
  static int list[5] = {1,2,3,4,5};
  static int table[2] [2] = {{11,12},
                             {21,22}};
  function1(list);
  function2(list);
  function3(table);
  exit(EXIT_SUCCESS);
  }

void function1(int list[])
  {
  register int index;

  for (index=0; index < 5; index++)
    {
    printf("list[%d] = %d\n", index, list[index]);
    }
  printf("\n");
```

```
    return;
    }
void function2(int *list)
    {
    register int index;

    for (index=4; index >= 0; index--)
        {
        printf("list[%d] = %d\n", index, *(list + index));
        }
    printf("\n");
    return;
    }


void function3(int table[] [2])
    {
    register int row, column;

    for (row = 0; row < 2; row++)
        {
        for (column= 0; column < 2; column++)
            {
            printf("%d ", table[row] [column]);
            }
        printf("\n");
        }
    return;
    }
```

The use of pointers to arrays can get a little bit complicated with multi-dimensional arrays but, if you need to use them, then the following list of equivalences should help to clarify matters.

list[i]	is equivalent to	*(list + i)
&list[i]	is equivalent to	(list + i)
table[i] [j]	is equivalent to	*(*(table +i) +j)
&table[i] [j]	is equivalent to	*(table +i) +j

There is a clear pattern to these equivalences and they can be extended to as many dimensions as required.

11.6 A chess board puzzle

The program queens uses most of the techniques described in this chapter to solve the problem of placing eight queens on a chess board so that no queen can be captured by any other queen. There are a total of 92 solutions to this problem but, because the chess board generates a great deal of symmetry, only eight of the solutions are unique. The other 84 solutions are transformations of the 8 unique solutions. The program queens generates all 92 solutions.

A chess queen can move along the rows, columns and diagonals of the board. The eight queens problem reduces to placing one queen on each row and column. The one dimensional, nine element array, column[9], is used in the program queens to store the row number on which a queen is placed for any column. The elements column[1] to column[8] are used to store the row position of the eight queens in each of the 8 columns of the chess board, the unused element, column[0], has to be available because a backtracking routine looks at the current column minus 1 and it is not possible to access a negatively subscripted array.

The program works by placing the first queen on column 1, row 1 of the chess board and then the next queen in the first available safe row in column 2, i.e. column 2, row 3 (column[2] = 3). The third queen is placed in the first available safe row in column three and so on until an impasse is reached and no more queens can be placed.

When an impasse is reached backtracking comes into play. The last safely positioned queen has to be moved into an alternative safe position. If an alternative can be found then the process of placing the queens can continue. If it still cannot continue then the backtracking goes back another column. Backtracking can and does go back to the first queen and the process continues until all the solutions are found.

```c
/*
 * file name: queens
 * solve the 8 queens puzzle
 */

#include <stdio.h>
#include <stdlib.h>

#if !defined(TRUE)
  #define TRUE 1
  #define FALSE 0
#endif

int main(void)
```

```
{
int test(int lastrow, int row, int column[]);
int display(int *column);
static int column[9] = {0,0,0,0,0,0,0,0,0};
int counter = 8;
int row = 0;
int flag = TRUE;
int lastrow;

while (TRUE)
  {
  if (flag) row++;
  flag = TRUE;
  column[row]++;
  if (row == 1) column[row] = counter--;
  if (!column[row]) break;
  if (column[row] > 8)
    {
    column[row] = 0;
    row--;
    flag = FALSE;
    }
  if (flag && row != 1)
    {
    lastrow = row - 1;
    flag = test(lastrow, row, column);
    }
  if (flag && row == 8) flag = display(column);
  }
exit(EXIT_SUCCESS);
}

int test(int lastrow, int row, int column[])
  {
  int result = TRUE;
  int lastcol, thisrow;

  do
    {
    lastcol = column[lastrow];
    thisrow = column[row];
    if ((thisrow == lastcol)
    || (thisrow == (lastcol + row - lastrow))
    || (thisrow == (lastcol - row + lastrow)))
```

```
        {
        result = FALSE;
        break;
        }
     lastrow--;
     }
   while (lastrow);
   return result;
   }

int display(int *column)
   {
   static int solution = 1;
   register int horizontal, vertical;
   char dummy;

   printf("\n Solution number %02d\n\n", solution++);
   for (vertical = 1; vertical < 9; vertical++)
     {
     for (horizontal = 1; horizontal < 9; horizontal++)
        {
        if (horizontal == *(column + vertical)) printf("@@
          ");
        else printf("[] ");
        }
     printf("\n");
     }
   printf("\nPress Return to continue");
   dummy = getchar();
   return FALSE;
   }
```

12

Character strings

12.1 char variables and arrays

A variable of type char can be used in C to store a single character. A single character is identified in a C program by enclosing the character in single quotes, for example 'A'. A character string is identified by enclosing the string in double quotes, for example "ABC". It is not possible to store a string of characters in a variable of type char because there is simply not enough room. A char variable can store only one character but the smallest character string, for example "A", stores two characters. The character string "A" is represented by the character 'A' and the null character (ASCII 0). The null character is used as an end-of-string marker byte.

Character strings are always terminated with a null marker byte so that a character string with a logical length of n bytes has an actual length of n+1 bytes. A single character can be stored in a variable of type char and a character string with a logical length of n bytes can be stored in a char array with n+1 elements.

12.2 Declaring char arrays

There are two ways of declaring an array for storing a string of characters. First of all by simply declaring a char array and secondly by using pointers to a char array.

A twenty element static char array can be declared with the following code

```
static char text[20];
```

This declaration reserves space for twenty characters and fills the array with null bytes. If the static char array is to be declared and initialised with any other characters then this can be done as shown in the program initchar.

```
/*
 * file name: initchar
 * declare and initialise a char array
 */

#include <stdio.h>
#include <stdlib.h>

int main(void)
  {
  static char text[] = "This is a character string";

  printf("Message = %s\n", text);
  exit(EXIT_SUCCESS);
  }
```

There are a number of important points to notice about this combined declaration and initialisation. The first point is that the array text is declared without specifying the size of the array. When a character array is declared and initialised in this way the compiler counts the number of characters, adds 1 for the null end-of-string marker byte and allocates the appropriate amount of space to the array. There is no need to count the number of characters in the string and then add 1 to work out the size of the required array. It is permissible to count the number of characters and specify the array size. For example

```
static char text[6] = "Hello";
```

In this case it is quite easy to count the number of characters and add 1 for the null marker byte, but it is also easy to get the count wrong with a long string. There is nothing to be gained by counting the characters in a string it is usually a good idea to get the compiler to do the work unless we want to allocate more than the minimum amount of memory required for the string. The following declaration reserves more than the minimum amount of space.

```
static char text[20] = "Hello";
```

In this case only 6 characters are required for the string, the unused elements in the char array are filled with null bytes.

The second important point to note is that a char array must have the storage class static, or external static, if it is to be initialised using any of the related methods illustrated above. An automatic char array cannot be initialised using these methods.

The last point is that the identifier of the array is a pointer to the array and this pointer is a constant. The value of a constant cannot be modified by a program.

12.3 Declaring char arrays with pointers

A second method of declaring a char array is to use a pointer. The program pointchar demonstrates declaring char arrays with pointers and multiple char arrays with arrays of pointers of type char. Notice that the array of pointers points to arrays of character strings. Character strings are not stored in arrays of pointers.

```
/*
 * file name: pointchar
 * using pointers to character strings
 */

#include <stdio.h>
#include <stdlib.h>

int main(void)
   {
   char *point[2];
   char *ptr = "Hello";

   printf("ptr points to %s at address %p\n", ptr, ptr);
   ptr = "How are you?";
   printf("ptr points to %s at address %p\n", ptr, ptr);
   point[0] = "message 1";
   point[1] = "message 2";
   printf("point[0] points to %s at address %p\n",
           point[0], point[0]);
   printf("point[1] points to %s at address %p\n",
           point[1], point[1]);
   exit(EXIT_SUCCESS);
   }
```

In this example the compiler stores the text of the string "Hello" as an array of six elements and assigns the address of the array to the pointer ptr. The pointer is a variable which can be modified by a program but the text is considered to be read only and must not be altered. The pointer ptr is altered in the program to point to the array which stores the string "How are you?". Only the address stored in the pointer is altered. The second string does not overwrite the first string. Both strings are created and assigned an address during compilation and, although you can alter the address stored in the pointer, you cannot alter the contents of character arrays created in this way.

When pointers with the default automatic storage class are used as demonstrated in the program pointchar then the pointer is created every time the function is called and lost when the function is returned. The array of characters is created during compilation and permanently stored in the application file. The pointer has the storage class automatic and not the string itself. This is a round about way of doing the same job as a static char array.

12.4 typedef

If we are not happy with the names given to data types by C then we can change the names of existing data types and define new data types with the compiler directive typedef. We could, for example, define a data type called STRING with the following code.

```
int main(void)
  {
  typedef char STRING[40];
  STRING name, address;

  /* statements */
  }
```

The symbolic data type STRING is used to declare variables which would normally be defined as type char. The following statements

```
typedef char STRING[40];
STRING name, address;
```

are equivalent to

```
char name[40], address[40];
```

If it is necessary to use pointers to char arrays then typedef can be used to define a symbolic pointer data type. For example

```
int main(void)
  {
  typedef char *STRPTR;
  STRPTR ptr1, ptr2;

  /* statements */
  }
```

In this example

```
typedef char *STRPTR;
STRPTR ptr1, ptr2;
```

is equivalent to

```
char *ptr1, *ptr2;
```

A typedef statement is written inside a function for a local type definition or outside the functions for a global type definition. Symbolic data types are usually typed in upper case to distinguish them from other data types. Using typedef to create symbolic data types is a common practice with structures and unions (chapter 13) but you can use typedef whenever it improves the legibility of your programs.

12.5 String operations

So far we have only declared, defined and initialised char arrays. When we want to perform operations on character strings it is necessary to use the string functions defined in the header files string.h and stdlib.h. We cannot use assignment statements with strings after they have been initialised. The following code will generate an error during compilation.

```
int main(void)
  {
  static char source[] = "source string";
  char destination[40];

  destination = source; /* error!! */
  }
```

There are over twenty functions available in the header file string.h, as well as the three string conversion functions atoi, atol and atof which are defined in the general purpose header file stdlib.h. You should consult your C manual for a full list and explanation of all the functions but the following programs demonstrate some of the more useful string functions.

12.5.1 strcpy

strcpy(string1, string2) is used to copy a string from memory pointed to by string2 into an area of memory pointed to by string1, stopping after the null character is copied. The string pointed to by string1 is returned. For example

```
/*
 * file name: strcpy
 * demonstrate the use of strcpy
 */
```

```
#include <stdio.h>
#include <string.h>
#include <stdlib.h>

int main(void)
  {
  static char source[] = "this is the source string";
  char destination[40];

  strcpy(destination, source);
  printf("Destination string = %s\n", destination);
  exit(EXIT_SUCCESS);
  }
```

There is a version of strcpy which begins with strn instead of str. strncpy(string1, string2, n) copies the first n characters from memory pointed to by string2 into memory pointed to by string1, truncating the copied string if necessary.

12.5.2 strcmp

strcmp(string1, string2) compares the strings pointed to by string1 and string2 and returns an integer which indicates how they compared. Zero is returned when the two strings are identical, if the string associated with string1 is lexicographically greater than the string associated with string2 then the number returned is greater than zero, and if the string associated with string1 is lexicographically less than the string associated with string2 then the number returned is less than zero.

```
/*
 * file name: strcmp
 * demonstrate the use of strcmp
 */

#include <stdio.h>
#include <string.h>
#include <stdlib.h>

int main(void)
  {
  static char a[] = "TEST STRCMP";
  static char b[] = "TEST STRCMP";
  static char c[] = "test STRCMP";
  static char d[] = "TEST strcmp";
  int result;
```

```
puts ("a = TEST SRTCMP");
puts ("b = TEST STRCMP");
puts ("c = test STRCMP");
puts ("d = TEST strcmp");
result = strcmp(a, b);
printf("result of strcmp(a, b) is %d\n", result);
result = strcmp(a, c);
printf("result of strcmp(a, c) is %d\n", result);
result = strcmp(a, d);
printf("result of strcmp(a, d) is %d\n", result);
result = strcmp(d, a);
printf("result of strcmp(d, a) is %d\n", result);
result = strcmp(c, d);
printf("result of strcmp(c, d) is %d\n", result);
result = strcmp(d, c);
printf("result of strcmp(d, c) is %d\n", result);
exit(EXIT_SUCCESS);
}
```

12.5.3 strlen

strlen(string) returns the number of characters in the string pointed to by string, not including the zero end-of-string byte. strlen returns the logical length of the character string.

```
/*
 * file name: strlen
 * demonstrate the use of strlen
 */

#include <stdio.h>
#include <string.h>
#include <stdlib.h>

int main(void)
  {
  static char a[] = "short";
  static char b[] = "a little bit longer";
  int result;

  result = strlen(a);
  printf("There are %d bytes in: %s\n", result, a);
```

```
result = strlen(b);
printf("There are %d bytes in: %s\n", result, b);
exit(EXIT_SUCCESS);
}
```

12.5.4 strcat

strcat(string1, string2) appends a copy of the string pointed to by string2 to the end of string pointed to by string1. It is important to ensure that sufficient memory is allocated to string1 to allow the string associated with string2 to be appended, otherwise the results are unpredictable.

```
/*
 * file name: strcat
 * demonstrate the use of strcat
 */

#include <stdio.h>
#include <string.h>
#include <stdlib.h>

int main(void)
  {
  static char first[40] = "part one ";
  static char second[] = "+ part two.";

  strcat(first, second);
  printf("Concatenated string = \"%s\"\n", first);
  exit(EXIT_SUCCESS);
  }
```

There is a version of strcat which begins with strn instead of str. strncat(string1, string2, n) appends a copy of the first n characters of the string associated with string2 to the end of the string associated with string1.

12.5.5 atoi and atol

atoi(string) performs an ASCII to integer conversion on the string pointed to by string. There is also an ASCII to long int conversion function called atol and an ASCII to double function called atof. The functions atoi, atol and atof are defined in the file stdlib.h and not in string.h

```
/*
 * file name: atoi
 * demonstrate the use of atoi and atol
 */

#include <stdio.h>
#include <stdlib.h>

int main(void)
   {
   static char first[] = "1.2345";
   static char second[] = "6789";
   int result;
   long answer;

   result = atoi(first);
   printf("atoi(\"1.2345\") = %d\n", result);
   result = atoi(second);
   printf("atoi(\"6789\") = %d\n", result);
   answer = atol(first);
   printf("atol(\"1.2345\") = %ld\n", answer);
   answer = atol(second);
   printf("atol(\"6789\") = %ld\n", answer);
   exit(EXIT_SUCCESS);
   }
```

12.5.6 atof

atof(string) performs an ASCII to double precision floating point conversion on the string pointed to by string. You should not attempt to use atof to make an ASCII to single precision floating point conversion. The function name is a little bit misleading and has its roots in earlier versions of C which permitted ASCII to single precision floating point conversions.

```
/*
 * file name: atof
 * demonstrate the use of atof
 */
#include <stdio.h>
#include <stdlib.h>

int main(void)
   {
```

```
static char first[] = "1.2345";
static char second[] = "6789";
double result;

result = atof(first);
printf("atof(\"1.2345\") = %f\n", result);
result = atof(second);
printf("atof(\"6789\") = %f\n", result);
exit(EXIT_SUCCESS);
}
```

12.6 sscanf and sprintf

The function sscanf can be used to read data from a char array in the same way that scanf reads data from the keyboard. The first argument passed to sscanf is an array pointer but in most other respects sscanf works in just the same way as scanf except, of course, that it takes formatted data from a char array instead of the keyboard buffer.

The general form for sscanf is

```
n = sscanf(array_pointer, control_string, pointers... )
```

The complementary function sprintf is used to write to a char array instead of to the VDU screen. Again the first argument passed to sprintf is an array pointer and in most other respects sprintf works in the same ways as printf, except that it writes to a char array instead of the VDU screen.

The general form for fprintf is

```
n = sprintf(array_pointer, control_string, data_items...
)
```

Both sscanf and sprintf are defined in stdio.h. These functions are demonstrated in the program sprintf.

```
/*
 * file name: sprintf
 * reading from, and writing to, arrays
 */

#include <stdio.h>
#include <stdlib.h>
```

```
#define cubed(x)  ((x)*(x)*(x))

int main(void)
  {
  char buffer[80] = "123";
  int cardinal;

  sscanf(buffer, "%d", &cardinal);
  sprintf(buffer, "%d cubed = %d", cardinal,
     cubed(cardinal));
  puts(buffer);
  exit(EXIT_SUCCESS);
  }
```

12.7 Reading character strings into a program

12.7.1 Using the standard i/o functions

The first, and most simple, method of reading and storing a string is to adapt and extend the techniques demonstrated so far. To do this you will need to define a static char array and read the string from the keyboard into that array.

```
/*
 * file name: read
 * reading data into a char array
 */

#include <stdio.h>
#include <stdlib.h>

int main(void)
  {
  char array[100];

  printf("Type a string : ");
  fgets(array, 99, stdin);
  printf("You typed : %s\n", array);
  printf("type another : ");
  gets(array);
  printf("You typed : %s\n", array);
  printf("and another : ");
  scanf("%99s", array);
```

```
printf("You typed : %s\n", array);
exit(EXIT_SUCCESS);
}
```

The program read uses the functions fgets, gets and scanf from the header file stdio.h to read the keyboard. Both fgets and scanf are limited to reading 99 characters but gets could overrun the 100 bytes reserved for the character array. The function scanf is described in detail in chapter six and for reasons explained in chapter six, it is a good idea to avoid using scanf whenever possible and to restrict yourself to fgets and gets to read data into char arrays.

The most useful function is fgets and the general form of fgets is

```
value = fgets(pointer, n, stream);
```

The function fgets reads up to n-1 characters from the file pointed to by stream into memory pointed to by pointer. In the program read the file pointed to by stream is stdin, the standard input file, the keyboard. Up to n-1 characters are read by fgets and so up to 98 characters can be read when n = 99. This leaves one byte free for the carriage return character and another byte free for the null end-of-string marker byte before all 100 bytes allocated to array[100] are used.

12.7.2 Memory allocation functions

malloc, calloc, realloc and free

If the length of character strings to be typed when a program is running is unknown to the programmer then another method of taking strings from the keyboard and storing them in memory can be employed. This method involves using the memory allocation and string operation functions.

In C, memory is allocated by calling one of two functions, either malloc or calloc, and the memory made available remains allocated until it is explicitly released by calling the complementary function free. Memory allocated by malloc or calloc can be extended or contracted with realloc before being released with free. If these functions are used with a suitable input buffer then only the minimum amount of space needs to use allocated for storing strings whose length is not known until the program is running.

When a number of character strings are to be taken from the user and stored in memory then a string buffer larger than the longest single string is defined and used as an input buffer. This buffer can be defined with the following code

```
auto char buffer[50];
```

In this case one would expect the longest string to be input into the buffer to be less than 50 characters including a carriage return and a null end-of-string marker byte. The storage class auto is used because there is no point in initialising the buffer. As well as having an input buffer it is also necessary to declare a pointer which will point to the first character of the final destination of the string. The string will be taken from the buffer and transferred to its final destination. If, for example, only one string is to be stored then the pointer can be declared as follows

```
char *text;
```

If ten strings are to be stored then either ten pointers, or an array of pointers with ten elements, can be declared. For example

```
char *text[10];
```

The function malloc can be used to allocate the memory for the final destination of the string and this function returns the type pointer to void. This does not mean pointer to nothing, it means that the address returned by malloc can be assigned to any pointer without having to cast the returned pointer into an appropriate type.

The functions malloc, calloc, realloc and free are all declared in the header file stdlib.h and this file must be included in the program. The function malloc takes one argument which must be an unsigned integer indicating how many bytes of storage to allocate. If, for example, we want to allocate sufficient space for 50 characters then we can use the following code

```
char *text;
text = malloc(50 * sizeof(char));
```

The pointer text stores the address of the first byte of the allocated memory. The memory locations can be referenced with text[0], text[1] and so on up to text[49] and used just as we would use a char array declared as text[50]. If successful malloc allocates memory but does not clear that memory. We can use malloc, calloc and realloc to create variable length arrays of any type. The following code can be used to allocate memory for an array of 50 double precision numbers.

```
double *decimal;
decimal = malloc(50 * sizeof(double));
```

The function calloc takes two arguments, the number of data elements and the size in bytes of each data element. The product of the two arguments taken by calloc is the same as the single argument taken by an equivalent call to malloc. The memory allocated by calloc is filled with null bytes. The following call is equivalent to the previous example.

```
double *decimal;
decimal = calloc(50, sizeof(double));
```

The function realloc takes two arguments, the address previously returned by either malloc or calloc and the new size for the allocated memory, in bytes. If the previous example needs to be increased to 100 numbers then the following code could be used.

```
unsigned int newsize;
char *decimal;

decimal = calloc(50, sizeof(double));
newsize = 100 * sizeof(double);
text = realloc(decimal, newsize);
```

The demonstration program malloc uses the function malloc but before this function is used to allocate memory for a string, that string has to be read into a buffer and its length measured with the function strlen. Be careful when using strlen because it returns the logical length of a string and does not include the end-of-string null marker byte. When we use malloc to allocate memory for a string we must add 1 to the length returned by strlen to accommodate the null marker byte.

The functions malloc, calloc and realloc return the value NULL (a pointer to the address zero) if they are unable to allocate sufficient contiguous memory. When sufficient memory has been allocated then the string can be copied from the buffer to its final destination using the function strcpy. This procedure can be repeated as many times as necessary using only one input buffer and just enough memory allocated for the final destination of the strings.

When the strings are finished with, the memory used to store them can be released with the function free. The function free takes as it argument the pointer to the memory allocated by malloc and returns the integer value zero if it is successful in releasing the memory.

This technique is much easier to implement than to explain and it is demonstrated in the program malloc which is used to input just one string. The demonstrated technique is much more useful when used to input multiple strings.

```
/*
 * file name: malloc
 * using malloc to allocate memory for a string
 */
#include <stdio.h>
#include <stdlib.h>
#include <string.h>
```

```
int main(void)
  {
  char buffer[50];
  char *text;
  unsigned int cardinal;
  printf("Type a short string : ");
  fgets(buffer, 49, stdin);
  cardinal = strlen(buffer) + 1;
  if ((text = malloc(cardinal * sizeof(char))) == NULL)
    {
    puts("malloc unable to allocate memory");
    exit(EXIT_FAILURE);
    }
  strcpy(text, buffer);
  printf("You typed : %s", text);
  free(text);
  exit(EXIT_SUCCESS);
  }
```

12.7.3 Reading arguments typed after the application file name

The last method of reading character strings from the keyboard uses the technique of reading arguments typed after the application file name. This technique is described in chapter two. You can use strcpy to transfer the text string from the argument to a char array or into memory set aside for the string by either malloc, calloc or realloc.

It is not possible to run programs which take a list of arguments after the application file name by double clicking on the application file icon and for this reason all programs using this method should provide an alternative method of input which allows the program to be run from the Desktop. The following programs demonstrate a suitable alternative and all the programs used to illustrate this book can be run by double clicking on an appropriate Desktop icon, either the application file icon or an obey file icon. Writing suitable obey files is described in chapter two.

The program arabic can read a roman number following the application file name and convert that number into an Arabic number, that is, an unsigned integer. There are seven symbols in the Roman notation and they represent the following integer values:

Symbol	Value
M	1000
D	500
C	100
L	50
X	10
V	5
I	1

The rules for representing an integer in Roman notation are

Rule 1

The characters in the Roman notation appear successively in decreasing order of value from left to right.

Rule 2

Some of the characters have to occur more than once with some numbers.

Rule 3

If any character is followed by a character of greater value then the value of the first character of that pair becomes negative.

Rule 4

The only characters that can precede one of greater value are C, X and I and they can only precede M or D, C or L, X or V respectively.

The program arabic uses these rules to convert any number written in upper case Roman notation into Arabic notation. The number should be less than or equal to MMMMCMXCIX, (4999 decimal). Compile and link the program and then run it by typing, For example

```
arabic MCMLXXXIX.
```

at the command line prompt, or from an obey file (a batch file), or by simply double clicking the application file icon.

```
/*
 * file name: arabic
 * convert roman to arabic numerals
 */

#include <stdio.h>
#include <string.h>
#include <stdlib.h>

int main(int argc, char *argv[])
  {
  int loop, pass, arabic, length;
  int cardinal = 0;
  int before = 5000;
  char letter, roman[20];
  static char list[] = "MDCLXVI";
```

```
  static int values[7] = {1000,500,100,50,10,5,1};

  if (argc != 2)
    {
    printf("Enter Roman number : ");
    gets(roman);
    }
  else strcpy(roman, argv[1]);
  length = strlen(roman);
  for (loop = 0; loop < length; loop++)
    {
    letter = roman[loop];
    arabic = 0;
    for (pass = 0; pass < 7; pass++)
      {
      if (letter == list[pass]) arabic = values[pass];
      }
    if (arabic == 0)
      {
      puts("Use upper case Roman numerals");
      exit(EXIT_FAILURE);
      }
    cardinal += arabic;
    if (arabic > before) cardinal -= (2 * before);
    before = arabic;
    }
  printf("%s = %d\n", roman, cardinal);
  exit(EXIT_SUCCESS);
  }
```

The reverse problem of converting Arabic notation into Roman notation is solved with the program roman. The argument should be an Arabic number (unsigned integer), less than or equal to 4999.

```
/*
 * file name: roman
 * convert arabic to roman numerals
 */

#include <stdio.h>
#include <stdlib.h>

int main(int argc, char *argv[])
  {
  int loop, arabic, cardinal;
```

```
int ordinal = 0;
static char roman[20], text[20];
static char list[] = "MDCLXVI";
static int listvals[7] = {1000,500,100,50,10,5,1};
static char before[] = "CCXXIII";
static int beforevals[7] = {100,100,10,10,1,1,1};
if (argc != 2)
  {
  printf("Enter Arabic number : ");
  fgets(text, 19, stdin);
  cardinal = atoi(text);
  }
else cardinal = atoi(argv[1]);
if (cardinal > 4999 || cardinal < 0)
  {
  puts("Integer range 0 - 4999");
  exit(EXIT_FAILURE);
  }
arabic = cardinal;
do
  {
  for (loop = 0; loop < 7; loop++)
    {
    if (listvals[loop] <= arabic)
      {
      roman[ordinal] = list[loop];
      ordinal++;
      arabic -= listvals[loop];
      break;
      }
    if (arabic >= (listvals[loop] - beforevals[loop]))
      {
      roman[ordinal] = before[loop];
      roman[ordinal+1] = list[loop];
      ordinal += 2;
      arabic += (beforevals[loop] - listvals[loop]);
      break;
      }
    }
  }
while (arabic);
printf("%d = %s\n", cardinal, roman);
exit(EXIT_SUCCESS);
}
```

Data Structures

13.1 Structures compared to arrays

There is a serious limitation imposed upon using arrays to store lists of data in memory because each element of an array must be of the same type. This can pose a problem when we want to store data items which naturally form a related unit but which contain individual items of different types such as character strings and integers. We cannot store both character strings and integers in the same array. An array can only store data items of one type.

When individual data items are brought together so that the data forms a single unit which represents the natural organisation of the data then this group is usually called a record. If you have used the Pascal programming language you will be familiar with the record data type. The C equivalent of the Pascal record data type is the structure data type.

The natural organisation of data stored in databases is represented by records. It is important to realise that although structures can be used to create records stored on disk there is no built-in link between structure data types and records stored on disk. C data structures are not the same as records stored on disk.

Data structures, also known as structured variables, are used in C to create new data types. When we use data structures we are not limited to using arrays in which all the elements are of the same type. Structured variables allow us to mix data of different types in the same structure.

13.2 Single structures

Consider one way in which the date can be written: 1 MARCH 1991. The date is composed of three data items which are not all the same type. The days and years are represented by integers and the month is represented by a character string.

If we want to store the date in an array we will have to store the day and year in the same data type as the month. We will have to use a char array because we cannot mix data types in an array. If, on the other hand, we define a data structure to deal with the same task then the month can be stored as a character string and the day and year as integers, all within the same data structure.

Not all the uses of data structures will be as simple as this example but even if we never use data structures directly we often use them indirectly because storing data from within a program onto disk uses data structures on our behalf. We must not let this mislead us into believing that disk records are the same as data structures, they are not the same, no matter how similar they seem.

13.3 Defining structures

The keyword struct is used to define a data structure. Using the date example described above, a structured variable can be defined in much the same way that other variables are declared. For example

```
int main(void)
  {
  struct date /* date is the tag of the structure template */
    {
    int day; /* the first member */
    char month[20]; /* the second member */
    int year; /* the third member */
    };

  /* statements */
  }
```

Defining a data structure does not reserve any memory for data. The keyword struct is used to define a template which describes the format for the data and to assign a identifier to the structure template. The identifier of the structure template is often called a tag and the structure can contain any data type, including other data structures.

The structure definition can be either global or local, depending on where the definition is made. In the outline program above the definition is local to the main function and it will not be usable in any other function within the same program. If the definition is made outside the functions in a program, usually in the global white space between the preprocessor statements and the first line of main, then the structure definition is global and available to all the functions in a program.

13.4 Declaring structures

After a data structure has been defined it can be used in a program just as any other data type can be used. If the structure defined above is to be used for only one date then a structured variable of type date can be declared and made available for storing information. For example

```
int main(void)
  {
  struct date
    {
    int day;
    char month[20];
    int year;
    };

  struct date david;
  /* the structured variable identifier is david */
  /* the structured variable type is date */

  /* statements */
  }
```

In this case a structured variable identified as david is declared as type date. When a variable is declared in this way then memory is allocated for the data to be stored in the structure. In this case 4 bytes will be available for the day, 20 bytes for the month and another 4 bytes for the year. The size of a structured variable can be found with the function sizeof.

```
/*
 * file name: howbig
 * find the number of bytes used by a structure
 */

#include <stdio.h>
#include <stdlib.h>

int main(void)
  {
  struct date
```

```
  {
  int day;
  char month[20];
  int year;
  };
struct date david;
int how_big = sizeof(david);

printf("Structure uses %d bytes\n", how_big);
exit(EXIT_SUCCESS);
}
```

It is possible to declare two or more variables using the same structure template if, for example, two dates are to be recorded. The following outline program uses a typedef declaration to create a symbolic data type DATE and to declare two variables of type DATE.

```
int main(void)
   {
   struct date
      {
      int day;
      char month[20];
      int year;
      };
   typedef struct date DATE;
   DATE david;
   DATE george;

   /* statements */
   }
```

The symbolic data type DATE is a structured variable of type date. The statements

```
typedef struct date DATE;
DATE david;
```

and

```
struct date david;
```

are equivalent. It is common practice to use typedef declarations with data structures because they make the source code easier to read and understand. In this case the two structured variables david and george are declared as symbolic type DATE and each structured variable will use 28 bytes.

13.5 Arrays of structures

When multiple data sets are stored it is more usual to use arrays of structures rather than multiple structured variables. The david and george structured variables used to illustrate the last example can be replaced with an array of structures. The program bigger uses an alternative method of declaring a symbolic type DATE with the typedef declaration at the head of the structure definition. This is the most commonly used method of defining symbolic data structure types because it involves less typing and it is easier to read.

```c
/*
 * file name: bigger
 * count the bytes used by an array of structures
 */

#include <stdio.h>
#include <stdlib.h>

int main(void)
  {
  typedef struct
    {
    int day;
    char month[20];
    int year;
    } DATE;
  DATE saints[2];
  int how_big = sizeof(saints);

  printf("Structure uses %d bytes\n", how_big);
  exit(EXIT_SUCCESS);
  }
```

The program bigger creates a structured array called saints which has two elements of the symbolic type DATE. The declaration

```c
DATE saints[2];
```

reserves memory for a one dimensional array with two elements of type DATE. Like all arrays, these elements are indexed 0 and 1, not 1 and 2. C will reserve 56 bytes for this structured array and it should be clear from this example that large structured arrays can use huge amounts of memory.

13.6 Accessing structures

After a structure has been declared it is accessed using the structure identifier, the period (or member) operator, and the member identifier. A structured variable david of type DATE can be accessed as shown in the program david. If you use the next few example programs it will be useful to know the following saints' days.

Saint David's Day	1st March
Saint Patrick's Day	17th March
Saint George's Day	23rd April
Saint Andrew's Day	30th November
Saint Stephen's Day	26th December

```c
/*
 * file name: david
 * using data structures
 */
#include <stdio.h>
#include <stdlib.h>

int main(void)
  {
  typedef struct
    {
    int day;
    char month[12];
    int year;
    } DATE;
  DATE david;
  char string[20];

  printf("\nEnter Saint David's day\n");
  printf("Day : ");
  gets(string);
  david.day = atoi(string);
  printf("Month : ");
  gets(david.month);
  printf("Year : ");
  gets(string);
  david.year = atoi(string);
  printf("%0.2d %s %d\n",
          david.day, david.month, david.year);
  exit(EXIT_SUCCESS);
  }
```

In this case the member david.month can be used just as any other character string would be used, and the members david.day and david.year can be used just as any other integers.

When structured arrays are used then the members of the array are identified using subscripts (indices) after the array identifier, not subscripts after the member identifier. In the program george the array identifier is saints. The member saints[0].month is the month of Saint David's day, and saints[1].day is the day of Saint George's day.

```
/*
 * file name: george
 * using structured arrays
 */

#include <stdio.h>
#include <stdlib.h>

int main(void)
  {
  typedef struct
    {
    int day;
    char month[20];
    int year;
    } DATE;
  DATE saints[2];
  char string[20];
  register int loop;

  for (loop = 0; loop < 2; loop++)
    {
    if (loop == 0)
      {
      printf("Enter Saint David's day\n");
      }
    else
      {
      printf("Enter Saint George's day\n");
      }
    printf("Day : ");
    gets(string);
    saints[loop].day = atoi(string);
    printf("Month : ");
```

```
      gets(saints[loop].month);
      printf("Year : ");
      gets(string);
      saints[loop].year = atoi(string);
      }
   printf("Saint David's day\n");
   printf("%0.2d %s %d\n",
            saints[0].day, saints[0].month,
          saints[0].year);
   printf("Saint George's day\n");
   printf("%d %s %d\n",
            saints[1].day, saints[1].month,
          saints[1].year);
   exit(EXIT_SUCCESS);
   }
```

The member saints[n].month is a char array and because it is an array we can also use subscripts on the member to identify elements of that array. For example the statement

```
   printf("First month, first character = %c\n",
     saints[0].month[0]);
```

can be used to display the first character of the first month which is stored in the zeroth element of the member identified as month[20] in the data structure template.

13.7 Defining and declaring structures

The sequence of defining a data structure template and declaring a structured variable can be shortened so that the structure is defined and declared at the same time. The following outline program defines a data structure and declares a local structured variable called andrew.

```
   int main(void)
     {
     struct            /* define a structure template */
       {
       int day;
       char month[20];
       int year;
       } andrew; /* declare the structured variable andrew */
     /* statements */
     }
```

There is no structure tag following the keyword struct in this example. The variable identifier andrew follows the closing brace of the template. Multiple variable identifiers can be declared using this method. To declare multiple variables we simply add the variable identifiers after the closing brace, separate the identifiers with commas and end the list with a semicolon. For example

```
int main(void)
  {
  struct
    {
    int day;
    char month[20];
    int year;
    } andrew, patrick;

  /* statements */
  }
```

13.8 Initialising structures

Just as it is possible to initialise other types of variables it is also possible to initialise structured variables. Whether a structured variable can be initialised follows the same rules as for an array variable. Only static and external structured variables can be initialised. The program stephen defines a symbolic data type called DATE and then uses the symbolic data type to declare and initialise a static structured variable called stephen.

```
/*
 * file name: stephen
 * declare and initialise a structure
 */

#include <stdio.h>
#include <stdlib.h>

int main(void)
  {
  typedef struct
    {
    int day;
    char *month;
    int year;
    } DATE;
  static DATE stephen = {26, "December", 1991};
```

```
printf("Saint Stephen's day is on the ");
printf("%d %s %d\n",
         stephen.day, stephen.month, stephen.year);
exit(EXIT_SUCCESS);
}
```

The same technique can be used to initialise an array of structures. For example

```
/*
 * file name: dates
 * declare and initialise an array of structures
 */

#include <stdio.h>
#include <stdlib.h>

int main(void)
  {
  typedef struct
    {
    int day;
    char *month;
    int year;
    } DATE;
  static DATE saints[2] = {{1, "March", 1991},
                           {23, "April", 1991}};
  printf("Saint David's Day is on the ");
  printf("%0.2d %s %d\n",
         saints[0].day, saints[0].month, saints[0].year);
  printf("Saint George's Day is on the ");
  printf("%d %s %d\n",
         saints[1].day, saints[1].month, saints[1].year);
  exit(EXIT_SUCCESS);
  }
```

The printf conversion specifier %0.2d makes printf display the number 1 as 01 so that Saint David's day is displayed as 01 March 1991. Conversion specifiers are described in chapter six.

13.9 Pointers to structures

Pointers can be used with structures just as with other data types. As with all data types, the & operator is used to indicate the address of a variable and the * operator is used to indicate the data stored in an address. Pointers to structures are defined and declared as shown below.

```
int main(void)
  {
  typedef struct
    {
    int day;
    char month[12];
    int year;
    } DATE;
  DATE saints[2];
  DATE *point; /* declare pointer to structure */
  point = &saints[0]; /* initialise pointer */

  /* statements */
  }
```

In this case a symbolic data type called DATE is defined and an array of structures of type DATE called saints[2] is declared. Then a pointer, called point, is declared. This is a pointer to a structure of type DATE. The pointer is assigned the address of the first member of the structured array saints.

A new operator called the membership operator can be used with pointers to identify the data stored in a member of an array of structures. The membership operator is formed from the minus sign followed by the greater than sign -> . Using the membership operator is demonstrated in the program pointst.

```
/*
 * file name: pointst
 * using pointers to structures
 */

#include <stdio.h>
#include <stdlib.h>

int main(void)
  {
  typedef struct
    {
    int day;
    char *month;
    int year;
```

```
    } DATE;
  static DATE saints[2] = {{1, "March", 1991},
                           {23, "April", 1991}};
    DATE *point;
    point = &saints[0]; /* point to first structure */
    printf("Saint David's Day is on the ");
    printf("%0.2d %s %d\n",
            point->day, point->month, point->year);
    point = &saints[1]; /* move pointer */
    printf("Saint George's Day is on the ");
    printf("%d %s %d\n",
            point->day, point->month, point->year);
    exit(EXIT_SUCCESS);
    }
```

The expression

```
  point->day
```

is equivalent to the expression

```
  (*point).day
```

but it is much more usual to use the membership operator rather than the period operator when dealing with pointers to structures.

13.10 Passing structures to functions

Structures can be passed to functions in just the same way as any other types of variables but this can use up huge amounts of memory and it is far better to pass a pointer to a structure rather than the structure itself. Passing pointers is more economical with memory usage and usually results in quicker execution times for the compiled program. The program passpoint demonstrates passing pointers to structures to functions.

```
/*
 * file name: passpoint
 * passing pointers to structures to functions
 */

#include <stdio.h>
#include <stdlib.h>

typedef struct
```

```
    {
    int day;
    char *month;
    int year;
    } DATE;
int main(void)
    {
    void display(DATE *st);
    static DATE saints[2] = {1, "March", 1991,
                              23, "April", 1991};

    display(&saints[0]); /* these two statements */
    display(saints); /* are equivalent */
    exit(EXIT_SUCCESS);
    }

void display(DATE *st)
    {
    printf("\nSaint David's Day is on the ");
    printf("%0.2d %s %d\n",
            st->day, st->month, st->year);
    st = &st[1];
    printf("Saint George's Day is on the ");
    printf("%d%s %d\n",
            st->day, st->month, st->year);
    return;
    }
```

Passing an entire data structure to a function rather than a pointer to a data structure is demonstrated in the program pass_struc.

```
/*
 * file name: pass_struc
 * passing structures to functions
 */

#include <stdio.h>
#include <stdlib.h>

typedef struct
    {
    int day;
    char month[10];
    int year;
```

```
} DATE;

int main(void)
  {
  DATE display(DATE david);
  static DATE david = {1, "March", 1991};
  static DATE patrick;
  patrick = display(david); /* pass entire structure */
    /* the returned structure is assigned to patrick */
  printf("Saint Patrick's Day is on the ");
  printf("%d %s %d\n",
          patrick.day, patrick.month, patrick.year);
  exit(EXIT_SUCCESS);
  }

DATE display(DATE david)
  {
  printf("Saint David's Day is on the ");
  printf("%0.2d %s %d\n",
          david.day, david.month, david.year);
  david.day = 17; /* move on to St. Patrick's day */
  return david;
  }
```

13.11 Dynamic allocation of memory

Memory can be allocated to structures dynamically, that is, allocated when the program is running rather than when the program is compiled. This can be a useful technique to use when we do not know the number of data items to be used by a program until the program is actually running. One way to approach the problem of not knowing how much data to store is to create an array of structures that is much bigger than we will ever need to use. A more elegant solution is to allocate memory as data items are added and to release memory when the data items are deleted.

The functions malloc and free dynamically reserve and release blocks of memory. These functions are described in chapter 12 but essentially, malloc reserves the number of bytes requested by an argument passed to the function and it returns the address of the first reserved location, or NULL if sufficient memory is not available. The function free is used to release the block of memory reserved by malloc. The address of the first reserved memory location is passed as an argument to free.

The function malloc returns a void pointer to the first byte of the reserved memory. The example program 'telephone' uses the expression:

```
point = malloc(sizeof(PHONE));
```

to allocate a block of memory the size of the symbolic data type PHONE and to store the address of the first byte in the pointer point, which is a pointer to data type PHONE. The program telephone is a very simple demonstration of the use of dynamic memory allocation. Memory is dynamically allocated using malloc and released with free.

```
/*
 * file name: telephone
 * dynamic allocation of memory
 */

#include <stdio.h>
#include <stdlib.h>

typedef struct
   {
   char name[40];
   char number[20];
   } PHONE;

int main(void)
   {
   PHONE *point;

   point = malloc(sizeof(PHONE));
   printf("Name : ");
   gets(point->name);
   printf("Phone number : ");
   gets(point->number);
   puts("You typed:");
   printf("%s %s\n", point->name, point->number);
   free(point);
   exit(EXIT_SUCCESS);
   }
```

13.12 Linked lists

The function malloc can be used to construct a linked list of structures. A linked list is a set of structures in which each structure contains a member which points to the next structure in the list. The structures are linked together by including the address of the next structure in the list. The structure template used in the program telephone can be modified to include a pointer to a structure of type phone.

```
struct phone
  {
  char name[40];
  char number[20];
  struct phone *next;
  };
```

This addition to the template does not include a structure of type phone as the third member of the template but a pointer to a structure of type phone. This pointer is used to point to the next structure in a linked list.

As well as every structure in a linked list having a member which points to the next structure, a program using a linked list must also have a pointer to the first structure in the list and mark the end of the list in some way. The program linklist uses a pointer to a structure of type phone called first to point to the first structure and stores NULL in the pointer in the last record allocated memory by malloc to indicate the end of the linked list.

When malloc is used to create the first structure in the linked list, the address returned by malloc is stored in the pointer first. The address stored in first is then assigned to the pointer current. This pointer is used by the program to point to the current structure in the linked list.

The program creates a linked list using a for loop. The function malloc is called every time a new record is created and returns the address of each new record into the pointer of the previous record. When the linked list is complete a NULL address is stored in the last pointer.

```
/*
 * file name: linklist
 * create a linked list with 3 members
 */

#include <stdio.h>
#include <stdlib.h>

struct phone
  {
  char name[40];
  char number[20];
  struct phone *next;
  };

int main(void)
```

```
{
register int loop;
struct phone *first, *current;

first = malloc(sizeof(struct phone));
current = first;
for (loop = 0; loop < 3; loop++)
  {
  printf("Name : ");
  gets(current->name);
  printf("Phone number : ");
  gets(current->number);
  current->next = malloc(sizeof(struct phone));
  current = current->next;
  }
current->next = NULL;
current = first;
printf("\nYou typed:\n");
while (current->next != NULL)
  {
  printf("%s %s\n", current->name, current->number);
  current = current->next;
  }
exit(EXIT_SUCCESS);
}
```

In this example malloc is used to dynamically allocate memory while the program is executing. The function free could also be used to dynamically release memory when records are deleted. If a record is to be deleted then the pointer to that record will have to be altered to point to the next record in the list and then the memory can be released by passing the address of the record to free. Any address returned by malloc can subsequently be passed to free to release the memory allocated by malloc.

13.13 Externally defined structures

A structure tm is defined in the header file time.h and this structure holds the components of the time in a format known as the broken-down time, that is, the time in seconds, minutes, hours, day of the month, month, year, day of the week, day of the year and daylight saving time. The structure tm is defined in time.h overleaf:

```
struct tm
  {
  int tm_sec;       /* seconds after the minute, 0 to 60
                       (0-60 allows for the occasional leap second) */
  int tm_min        /* minutes after the hour, 0 to 59 */
  int tm_hour       /* hours since midnight, 0 to 23 */
  int tm_mday       /* day of the month, 0 to 31 */
  int tm_year       /* years since 1900 */
  int tm_wday       /* days since sunday, 0 to 6 */
  int tm_yday       /* days since January 1, 0 to 365 */
  int tm_isdst      /* daylight saving flag */
  };
```

There are quite a number of functions in time.h which use this structure and it is possible to use these functions to display the time in either a user defined format or a fixed format.

The data type time_t is defined in time.h and used to represent the time as a number. The function time takes the address of a variable of type time_t as an argument and returns the calendar time in seconds. The following code declares a variable timer of type time_t and assigns the calendar time to timer.

```
#include <time.h>

int main(void)
  {
  time_t timer;
  time(&timer);

  /* statements */
  }
```

The function localtime converts the calendar time as returned by time into a broken-down time expressing the local time. The following code makes the broken-down local time available in the structure local.

```
#include <time.h>

int main(void)
  {
  struct tm local;
  time_t timer;

  time(&timer);
  local = *localtime(&timer);

  /* statements */
  }
```

The function strftime takes the broken-down time as an argument and formats a character string which displays the time and date to a user defined format. The general form of strftime is

```
strftime(array, max_size, control_string, time_pointer)
```

The first argument is char array large enough to take the formatted output from the function. No more than max_size characters are sent to the array. The control string consists of zero or more conversion specifiers and ordinary characters which format the characters sent to the array and time_pointer points to a structure of type tm which contains the broken-down time.

The following conversion specifiers can be used in the control string to format the data sent to the char array by strftime.

Specifier	*Meaning*
%a	abbreviated weekday name %A
	full weekday name
%b	abbreviated month name
%B	full month name
%c	date and time
%d	day of the month, 00 to 31
%H	hour, 24 hour clock, 00 to 23
%I	hour, 12 hour clock, 01 to 12
%j	day of the year, 000 to 366
%m	month, 01 to 12
%M	minute, 00 to 61
%p	AM or PM, associated with 12 hour clock
%S	second, 00 to 61
%U	week number of the year, 00 to 53 (Sunday as first day of the week)
%w	weekday, 0 (Sunday) to 6 (Saturday)
%W	week number of the year, 00 to 53 (Monday as first day of the week)
%x	date
%X	time
%y	year without century, 00 to 99
%Y	year with century, e.g. 1991
%Z	time zone name or no character if not available
%%	display %

If successful strftime returns the number of characters placed in the char array, including the null end-of-string marker byte, otherwise it returns zero. Using all these functions and the function ctime is demonstrated in the program time.

The function ctime is defined in time.h and it returns the time in a locally defined format.

```
/*
 * file name: time
 * using the time.h functions
 */

#include <stdio.h>
#include <stdlib.h>
#include <time.h>

int main(void)
  {
  struct tm local;
  time_t timer;
  char string[60];

  time(&timer);
  local = *localtime(&timer);
  strftime(string, 60, "%I:%M:%S %p, %A %d %B %Y",
    &local);
  printf("strftime gives: %s\n", string);
  printf("ctime gives: %s", ctime(&timer));
  exit(EXIT_SUCCESS);
  }
```

13.14 Bit fields

It is possible for structures to have members with their size expressed in bits. Such members are known as bit fields. The following structure defines a datatype BITFIELD with five members bithuge, bitbig, bitmed, bitsmall and bittiny which are bit fields of 32, 24, 8, 4 and 2 bits respectively.

```
typedef struct
  {
  unsigned int bithuge: 32,
               bitbig: 24,
               bitmed: 8,
               bitsmall: 4,
               bittiny: 2;
  } BITFIELD;
```

Bit fields are similar to other structure members except that the declaration specifies the maximum number of bits to be stored in the member. In the program bitfield the member bitsmall is only 4 bits wide and can only store an integer in the range 0-15, the member bittiny is only 2 bits wide and can only store integers in the range 0-3. Because bit fields can be smaller than one byte, more than one bit field may be stored in one byte and for this reason the bitfield members cannot be uniquely identified by their address. For obvious reasons the "address of" operator & must not be used with bit fields.

```
/*
 * file name: bitfield
 * structure containing bitfields
 */

#include <stdio.h>
#include <stdlib.h>

int main(void)
  {
  char buffer[20];
  typedef struct
    {
    unsigned int bithuge: 32,
                 bitbig: 24,
                 bitmed: 8,
                 bitsmall: 4,
                 bittiny: 2;
    } BITFIELD;
  BITFIELD bitza;
    printf("Enter 32 bit integer : ");
    /* range 0 - 4294967295 */
    bitza.bithuge = atoi(gets(buffer));
    printf("Enter 24 bit integer : ");
    /* range 0 - 16777215 */
    bitza.bitbig = atoi(gets(buffer));
    printf("Enter 8 bit integer : ");
    /* range 0 - 255 */
    bitza.bitmed = atoi(gets(buffer));
    printf("Enter 4 bit integer : ");
    /* range 0 - 15 */
    bitza.bitsmall = atoi(gets(buffer));
    printf("Enter 2 bit integer : ");
    /* range 0 - 3 */
    bitza.bittiny = atoi(gets(buffer));
```

```
printf("bitza.bithuge = %d\n", bitza.bithuge);
printf("bitza.bitbig = %d\n", bitza.bitbig);
printf("bitza.bitmed = %d\n", bitza.bitmed);
printf("bitza.bitsmall = %d\n", bitza.bitsmall);
printf("bitza.bittiny = %d\n", bitza.bittiny);
exit(EXIT_SUCCESS);
}
```

When data is stored in a four bit wide bit field only the 4 least significant bits are actually stored. If, for example, we try to store the number 55 in a four bit wide bit field then the number 7 will be stored. This is because decimal 55 is binary 110111, a six bit number. The four least significant bits of 110111 are 0111 which is the decimal number 7. The largest number that can stored in a four bit wide bitfield is binary 1111, i.e. decimal 15.

13.15 Unions

A union is equivalent to a variant record in Pascal and is another special data type that can be defined and used in C. A union is defined and declared in the same way as a structure but, unlike a structure, all the members of a union are stored at the same address. For this reason a union can only store the data for one of its members at a time. Unions can be used in the same way as structures and they can store the data for any of the members – but remember – only one member at any time.

A variable declared as a union data type can be used to hold any valid C data type including structures or other unions. The only restriction imposed upon a union is that only one data type at a time can be assigned to the union.

Tags can be associated with unions to create templates for unions without actually reserving any memory for the union. These templates can then be used in exactly the same way as structure templates. Unions can be members of structures and arrays, or structures and arrays can be members of unions.

A union is defined and declared in the same way as a structure except that the reserved word union is used in place of the reserved word struct. For example, the declaration

```
union
  {
  int cardinal;
  double decimal;
  char letter;
  char *text;
  } info;
```

creates the union identified as info which at any time can store a single member, either an integer variable, info.cardinal, a floating point variable, info.decimal, a character variable, info.letter, or a pointer to a character string, info.text. The union info reserves sufficient memory to allocate its largest data type, in this case a double precision floating point variable. The memory reserved for the union can then be referenced by appropriate variable identifiers depending on the data type currently using the memory allocated to the union.

The individual union members are referenced using the same notation as structure members. If, for example, an integer variable is stored in the memory allocated to the union then the variable is referenced by info.cardinal, if the union is used to point to a character string then the string is referenced by info.text, and so on.

Because the same area of memory is used to store variables of different types it is necessary to keep track of the data type currently stored in the union. This is demonstrated in the program union which uses the character stored in the char variable flag to indicate the data type stored in the union info.

```
/*
 * file name: union
 * demonstrate unions
 */

#include <stdio.h>
#include <stdlib.h>
#include <string.h>

int main(void)
   {
   char flag;
   char alphabet[10];
   typedef union
      {
      int cardinal;
      double decimal;
      char letter;
      char *text;
      } DATA;
   DATA info;
```

```
printf("Size of union = %d bytes\n", sizeof(info));
puts("Choose:");
puts("1: store integer 123 in union");
puts("2: store decimal number 4.56 in union");
puts("3: store character x in union");
puts("4: point to alphabet");
printf("Press 1-4 : ");
flag = getchar();
switch(flag)
  {
  case '1':
    {
    info.cardinal = 123;
    break;
    }
  case '2':
    {
    info.decimal = 4.56;
    break;
    }
  case '3':
    {
    info.letter = 'x';
    break;
    }
  case '4':
    {
    strcpy(alphabet, "abc...xyz");
    info.text = alphabet;
    break;
    }
  default:
    {
    puts("Use 1-4 only");
    exit(EXIT_FAILURE);
    }
  }
switch(flag)
  {
  case '1':
    {
    printf("%d stored in union\n", info.cardinal);
    break;
    }
```

```
    case '2':
      {
      printf("%f stored in union\n", info.decimal);
      break;
      }
    case '3':
      {
      printf("%c stored in union\n", info.letter);
      break;
      }
    case '4':
      {
      printf("union pointing to %s\n", info.text);
      break;
      }
    }
  exit(EXIT_SUCCESS);
  }
```

We can do anything with unions that can be done with structures except store more than one member at a time. Storing only one member does result in some memory saving when compared with structures because only sufficient memory for the largest member is allocated to the union, but this has to be weighed against the extra coding need to keep track of the data currently stored in the union.

14

Disk data Files

14.1 Data files

The data we make available to a program can be defined internally within the program, entered as arguments typed after the application file name, entered interactively during program execution, or made available from data files on a storage medium such as a disk. A data file is any collection of information stored under a unique file name on any storage medium. Data files may be stored in the computer's memory in RAM disks or made available on a remote storage device accessed via a network but the most commonly used storage medium is the disk data file. This chapter focuses on disk data files but the same techniques are used whatever the storage medium.

It is possible for a C program to write to and read from data files stored on a disk or any other storage medium. The data should be thought of as logical records and there is no need to be concerned with the physical mechanism of storage. It doesn't matter how many bytes there are in a disk sector and it doesn't even matter if we don't know what the term disk sector means. All that really matters is that there is enough space on a disk to store the data we want to use.

Because data is stored in logical records it is necessary to understand what this means. If, for example, we intend to store the names and addresses of a number of people on disk then the entire collection of names and addresses is called a file or, more commonly, a data file. The data associated with each individual in the file is called a record, the components of each record (the name, address, telephone number and so on) are called fields and every field will contain a number of characters.

Data is written to or read from files either as records, or as fields or as individual bytes and there are C functions defined in the header file stdio.h to deal with all these types of data transfer.

14.2 Opening a file

Before a file can be used it must be opened and after is has been used it must be closed. Opening a file using the function fopen establishes a link between the program and the data file, sets up the necessary control variables and creates a buffer for the file. The function fopen returns the starting address of a structure of type FILE which is used to write to and read from the data file. The type FILE (always in upper case) is a symbolic data type defined in the header file stdio.h and FILE should be regarded as a reserved word.

Before using fopen you need to declare a pointer to an object of type FILE. A pointer to an object of type FILE is known as a file pointer or a stream. The following code can be used to declare a file pointer fpoint and then initialise fpoint by assigning the value returned by the function fopen.

```
#include <stdio.h>

int main(void)
  {
  FILE *fpoint;

  fpoint = fopen("data_store", "w");

  /* statements */
  }
```

The general form of the function fopen is

```
file_pointer = fopen(file_name, mode)
```

The file name can include a full pathname and the mode determines the type of access that can be made to the file after it has been opened. The access types, or modes, are

Mode	Meaning
r	open text file for read only, the file must exist
w	create text file for write only
a	open text file for append (write at end of file)
rb	open binary file for read only
wb	create binary file for write only
ab	open binary file for append

r+	open text file for update (read and write)
w+	create text file for update
a+	open text file for append update
r+b or rb+	open binary file for update
w+b or wb+	create binary file for update
a+b or ab+	open binary file for append update

Files opened in read mode make their data available as input to a program and files opened in either write or append mode can be used to store data from a program. The difference between a file opened in write mode and one opened in append mode is in where the data sent to the file is placed. In write mode the data is written at the beginning of the file, deleting any existing file. In append mode the data is written on to the end of any existing file. The update (read and write) mode is a combination of the read and write modes.

All files are opened in either the default text mode or binary mode. In text mode both the characters "123" and the integer 123 are stored as the characters "123". In binary mode the characters "123" are stored as "123" but the integer 123 is stored as the four byte internal representation of the integer. The data stored in text mode can be formatted in the file in the same way that text is formatted on the screen using control characters such as newline, backspace and so on. Only the printable subset of characters is stored in text mode and the character Ctrl Z is used as an end of file marker. Using the binary mode will allow us to store bytes with the complete range of values from 0 to 255. Ctrl Z can be stored as data in binary mode.

The fopen parameters file_name and mode can be typed as strings in quotes. If the file name is stored in a char array then the array identifier can be used without quotes as the first argument.

If the function fopen fails to open a file it returns the value assigned to the macro NULL. It is a good idea to test the value returned by fopen. The following code can be used to open a file and test the value returned by fopen.

```
#include <stdio.h>
#include <stdlib.h>

int main(void)
  {
  FILE *fpoint;
  static char filename[] = "data_store";

  if ((fpoint = fopen(filename, "r")) == NULL)
    {
```

```
      puts("Failed to open file");
      exit(EXIT_FAILURE);
      }
   /* statements */
   }
```

14.3 Closing a file

When we have finished using a data file we must close the file before exiting the program. This will ensure that the file is up to date with all the data written from the file buffer to the file. Closing a file can also be used to release the file buffer so that another file can use it if required. The function fclose is used to close a file opened with fopen. The general form of fclose is

```
  n = fclose(file_pointer)
```

It is important to notice that the file pointer is used to close the file and not the file name. The function fclose returns the value zero if the file closes properly and the value assigned to the macro EOF if it fails. The value returned by fclose can be tested as shown below.

```
#include <stdio.h>
#include <stdlib.h>

int main(void)
   {
   FILE *fpoint;

   fpoint = fopen("data_store","w")

   /* statements */

   if (fclose(fpoint) != 0)
      {
      puts("Failed to close file");
      exit(EXIT_FAILURE);
      }
   exit(EXIT_SUCCESS);
   }
```

One reason for always using exit to return control from a program to the operating system is that exit will close any open files and prevent the loss of data that might occur if a file is left open when the program returns.

14.4 Writing to and reading from text files

14.4.1 fprintf and fscanf

The functions used to write to and read from text files are very similar to those used to display information on the screen and to input data from the keyboard. The file equivalents of printf and scanf are called fprintf and fscanf. These functions include an argument for the file pointer but in every other respect they are the same as their non-file equivalent functions. Numbers are converted to ASCII by fprintf and the ASCII representation of a number is converted back by fscanf. The general form for fprintf is

```
n = fprintf(file_pointer, control_string, data_items... )
```

The function fprintf returns the number of characters transmitted or a negative value if an output error occurs.

The general form for fscanf is

```
n = fscanf(file_pointer, control_string, pointers... )
```

The value returned by fscanf is equal to the number of data items read and assigned to variables. This can be fewer than expected or even zero if an error occurs. The function returns the value EOF if an input error occurs before any conversion.

The functions fprintf and fscanf can be used after a file is opened with fopen and before it is closed with fclose. The function fprintf is demonstrated in the following program.

```
/*
 * file name: fprintf
 * demonstrate the use of fprintf
 */

#include <stdio.h>
#include <stdlib.h>

int main(void)
  {
  FILE *fpoint;
  char c = 'C';
  int i = 1234;
  double d = 5.6789;
```

```
if ((fpoint = fopen("data_store","w")) == NULL)
  {
  puts("Failed to open file data_store");
  exit(EXIT_FAILURE);
  }
else puts("File data_store opened");
if (fprintf(fpoint, "%c %d %lf ", c, i, d) < 0)
  {
  puts("Error using fprintf");
  exit(EXIT_FAILURE);
  }
else puts("fprintf successful");
if (fclose(fpoint) == 0) puts("File data_store closed");
else
  {
  puts("Failed to close file data_store");
  exit(EXIT_FAILURE);
  }
exit(EXIT_SUCCESS);
}
```

When fscanf is used to read data from a file it will return the value EOF if an attempt is made to read beyond the end of the data file and we can check for EOF when using fscanf. There is another method of checking if the end of a file has been reached. The macro feof returns the value true (non-zero integer) if the end of the file has been reached or false (integer zero) if it has not yet been reached. Suitable code for making this check is included in the program fscanf which also demonstrates how the data written to the file data_store by the program fprintf can be read with the function fscanf.

```
/*
 * file name: fscanf
 * demonstrate the use of fscanf and feof
 */

#include <stdio.h>
#include <stdlib.h>

int main(void)
  {
  FILE *fpoint;
  char c;
  int i;
  double d;
```

```
if ((fpoint = fopen("data_store", "r")) == NULL)
   {
   puts("Failed to open file data_store");
   exit(EXIT_FAILURE);
   }
else puts("File data_store opened");
if (fscanf(fpoint,"%c %d %lf ", &c, &i, &d) != 3)
   {
   puts("Error using fscanf");
   exit(EXIT_FAILURE);
   }
else puts("fscanf successful");
if(feof(fpoint)) puts("End of file reached");
if (fclose(fpoint) == 0) puts("File data_store closed");
else
   {
   puts("Failed to close file data_store");
   exit(EXIT_FAILURE);
   }
printf("c = %c\n", c);
printf("i = %d\n", i);
printf("d = %f\n", d);
exit(EXIT_SUCCESS);
}
```

If you need to know any more about using fprintf and fscanf then go back to chapter six and remember that everything said about printf and scanf also applies to fprintf and fscanf. The function printf is a special case of fprintf that defaults to the standard output device, stdout, the VDU screen. The function scanf is a special case of the function fscanf, one which defaults to the standard input device, stdin, the keyboard.

It was mentioned in chapter six that the function scanf is unsuitable for keyboard input but that it is suitable for machine formatted input. Data files are a good example of machine formatted input and the function fscanf is well suited to reading data from files that have been written to using fprintf. The functions fprintf and fscanf truly complement one another but the same cannot be said for printf and scanf.

14.4.2 fputs and fgets

Just as printf and scanf are special cases of fprintf and fscanf respectively, the functions puts and gets are also special cases of the general functions fputs and fgets.

The file equivalents of puts and gets are fputs and fgets. The file functions again use an extra argument for the file pointer. The general form of fputs is

```
    n = fputs(array_pointer, file_pointer)
```

The function fputs returns EOF if a write error occurs, otherwise it returns a positive value. The general format of fgets is

```
  array_pointer = fgets(array_pointer, no_of_chars, file_poin-
      ter)
```

The function fgets returns the value NULL if an error occurs during reading. Notice that with both string functions the file pointer is the last argument.

The function fputs writes the contents of the char array pointed to by array_pointer to the file pointed to by file_pointer. This function does not send a new line character or a null character to mark the end of the text string. The function fputs is demonstrated in the program fputs which stores 16 bytes in the file data_file.

```
/*
 * file name: fputs
 * demonstrate the use of fputs
 */

#include <stdio.h>
#include <stdlib.h>

int main(void)
  {
  FILE *fpoint;
  int cardinal;
  static char message[] = "This is it folks";

  if ((fpoint = fopen("data_file", "w")) == NULL)
    {
    puts("Failed to open file data_file");
    exit(EXIT_FAILURE);
    }
  else puts("File data_file opened");
  if (cardinal = fputs (message, fpoint) , cardinal ==
    EOF)
    {
    puts("Error using fputs");
    exit(EXIT_FAILURE);
    }
  else printf("fputs returned %d\n", cardinal);
  if (fclose(fpoint) == 0) puts("File data_file closed");
```

```
else
   {
   puts("Failed to close file data_file");
   exit(EXIT_FAILURE);
   }
exit(EXIT_SUCCESS);
}
```

The function fgets reads from the file pointed to by file_pointer into a char array pointed to by array_pointer until either a new line character is read, or until the end of the file is reached, or until the no_of_chars minus 1 is read. A null character is written immediately after the last character read into the array. The function returns NULL if the end of file is reached.

The use of the function fgets is demonstrated in the program fgets which reads the 16 bytes written to the file data_file by the program fputs. Notice that the function fgets specifies 17 characters because fgets reads up to the number of characters minus 1.

```
/*
 * file name: fgets
 * demonstrate the use of fgets
 */

#include <stdio.h>
#include <stdlib.h>

int main(void)
   {
   FILE *fpoint;
   char message[40];

   if ((fpoint = fopen("data_file", "r")) == NULL)
      {
      puts("Failed to open file data_file");
      exit(EXIT_FAILURE);
      }
   else puts("File data_file opened");
   if (fgets (message, 17, fpoint) == NULL)
      {
      puts("Error using fgets");
      exit(EXIT_FAILURE);
      }
   else puts("fgets used successfully");
   if (feof(fpoint)) puts("end of file reached");
```

```
if (fclose(fpoint) == 0) puts("File data_file closed");
else
   {
   puts("Failed to close file data_file");
   exit(EXIT_FAILURE);
   }
printf("Message = %s\n", message);
exit(EXIT_SUCCESS);
}
```

14.4.3 fgetc and fputc

The file equivalents of getchar and putchar are fgetc and fputc respectively. As you might now expect both fgetc and fputc work like their counterparts getchar and putchar except that the new functions include a file pointer. The general form of fgetc is

```
character = fgetc(file_pointer)
```

The function fgetc returns the next character read from the file pointed to by file_pointer. It returns EOF if the end of file is reached or if an error occurs.

The general form of fputc is

```
n = fputc(character, file_pointer)
```

The function fputc returns the character written to the file pointed to by file_pointer. It returns EOF if an error occurs.

The function ungetc, which is used to move the file position back one character, it is not the opposite of fgetc and certainly not the same as fputc which writes a character to a file. The function ungetc is one of a number of functions which are used to move the file position around a file and to allow programmers to randomly access files opened with fopen.

The use of the functions fgetc and fputc is demonstrated in the program duplic8 which uses files opened in binary mode to duplicate any file, text or binary.

```
/*
 * file name: duplic8
 * demonstrate fgetc and fputc
 */

#include <stdio.h>
#include <stdlib.h>
```

```
#include <string.h>

#if !defined(TRUE)
  #define TRUE 1
#endif

int main(int argc, char *argv[])
  {
  int byte;
  char first[60], second[60];
  FILE *source, *destination;

  if (argc != 3)
    {
    printf("Enter source file name : ");
    gets(first);
    printf("Enter destination file name : ");
    gets(second);
    }
  else
    {
    strcpy(first, argv[1]);
    strcpy(second, argv[2]);
    }
  if ((source = fopen(first, "rb")) == NULL)
    {
    printf("\nUnable to open %s\n", first);
    exit(EXIT_FAILURE);
    }
  else printf("\n%s opened\n", first);
  if ((destination = fopen(second, "wb")) == NULL)
    {
    printf("Unable to open %s\n", second);
    exit(EXIT_FAILURE);
    }
  else printf("%s opened\n\n", second);
/*
 * if the variable byte is declared as type char then
 * this commented out code must be used instead of
 * the more elegant while loop which follows it.
 *
 *     while (TRUE)
 *        {
```

```
*        byte = fgetc(source);
*        if (feof(source)) break;
*        fputc(byte, destination);
*        }
*/
    while(byte = fgetc(source) , byte != EOF)
      {
      fputc(byte, destination);
      }
    printf("end of file %s\n\n", first);
    if (fclose(source) == 0) printf("%s closed\n", first);
    else
      {
      printf("Failed to close %s\n", first);
      exit(EXIT_FAILURE);
      }
    if (fclose(destination) == 0) printf("%s closed\n",
     second);
    else
      {
      printf("Failed to close %s\n", second);
      exit(EXIT_FAILURE);
      }
    exit(EXIT_SUCCESS);
    }
```

The program duplic8 can be used with both text files and binary files. This means that the program can be used to duplicate both C source code files and C object files.

Binary files are sometimes referred to as unformatted files because they do not have a line structure like text files. You cannot load a binary file into a word processor or simply print it on a line printer. The program duplic8 is a special case which deals with text files as if they are binary files. In general you should not open text files as binary files or vice versa.

14.5 Binary files

Binary files are always opened with a 'b' as part of the mode argument passed to fopen.

```
fpoint = ("bin_file", "wb");
```

In this case the file bin_file is created if it does not exist and its contents are erased if the file does exist. The file is opened for write only in binary mode.

There are two functions, fwrite and fread, which are used to store and read data in binary format. These functions provide an efficient way of storing numbers in a binary file because they both use the internal representation of numbers used by the computer itself and no conversion to or from character strings is necessary when they are used. This increase in efficiency can be worthwile when large arrays of numbers or complicated data structures are used in a program.

The general form of fwrite is

```
n = fwrite(pointer, size, no_of_items, file_pointer)
```

and the general form of the complementary function fread is

```
n = fread(pointer, size, no_of_items, file_pointer)
```

Both functions return the number of data items written to the file or read from the file. The value zero is returned if nothing can be written or read.

The first argument passed to fwrite and fread is the address of the first byte of memory which contains the data to be written by fwrite or the address of the first byte of the memory to be used to store the data read by fread. If, for example, the data item to be written to disk is an integer, i, then the first argument passed to fwrite will be &i, if an array declared as list[10] is to be used to receive data from disk then the first argument passed to fread will be the pointer list, and so on.

The second argument passed to fwrite and fread is the number of bytes needed for each data item. Because this may vary from one version of C to another you should use the sizeof operator to determine the required number. The third argument is the number of data items to be written or read and the last argument is the file pointer returned by fopen.

The use of the function fwrite is demonstrated in the program fwrite. This program is used to write the contents of an array of double precision floating point numbers to a binary file called bin_file in the currently selected directory.

```
/*
 * file name: fwrite
 * demonstrate the use of fwrite
 */

#include <stdio.h>
#include <stdlib.h>

int main(void)
   {
```

```
   FILE *fpoint;
   double list[4] = {1.2, 2.3, 3.4, 4.5};

   if ((fpoint = fopen("bin_file", "wb")) == NULL)
     {
     puts("Failed to open file bin_file");
     exit(EXIT_FAILURE);
     }
   else puts("File bin_file opened");
   if (fwrite(list, sizeof(double), 4, fpoint) != 4)
     {
     puts("Error using fwrite");
     exit(EXIT_FAILURE);
     }
   else puts("fwrite successful");
   if (fclose(fpoint) == 0) puts("File bin_file closed");
   else
     {
     puts("Failed to close file bin_file");
     exit(EXIT_FAILURE);
     }
   exit(EXIT_SUCCESS);
   }
```

The data written to the binary file bin_file can be read from disk with the complementary program fread.

```
/*
 * file name: fread
 * demonstrate the use of fread
 */

#include <stdio.h>
#include <stdlib.h>

int main(void)
  {
  FILE *fpoint;
  double list[4];
  register int loop;

  if ((fpoint = fopen("bin_file", "rb")) == NULL)
    {
    puts("Failed to open file bin_file");
```

```
      exit(EXIT_FAILURE);
      }
   else puts("File bin_file opened");
   if (fread(list, sizeof(double), 4, fpoint) != 4)
      {
      puts("Error using fread");
      exit(EXIT_FAILURE);
      }
   else puts("fread successful");
   if (feof(fpoint))
      {
      puts("Error! end of file read");
      exit(EXIT_FAILURE);
      }
   if (fclose(fpoint) == 0) puts("File bin_file closed");
   else
      {
      puts("Failed to close file bin_file");
      exit(EXIT_FAILURE);
      }
   for(loop = 0; loop < 4; loop++)
      {
      printf("list[%d] = %f\n", loop, list[loop]);
      }
   exit(EXIT_SUCCESS);
   }
```

The file produced by the program fwrite stores the elements of the array in the same format as in the computer's memory. We cannot examine the contents of the binary file with a text editor or print the file. We can use a text editor or a printer to examine the contents of a file when fprintf is used to create a text file to store the same information. It is a good idea to avoid using fwrite and fread instead of fprintf and fscanf unless increased efficiency is important. Programs using fwrite and fread will compile on any ANSI compiler but the data files produced by these functions are not portable from one machine to another.

14.6 Passing file pointers to functions

File pointers can be passed to functions using the same rules as for any other arguments. The file pointer should be declared in both the function prototype and the function definition as a pointer to an object of type FILE. This is illustrated in the following outline program. When control is passed to the function demo the file pointer fpointer can be used just as the pointer fpoint is used in main and both pointers point to the file data_store.

```
#include <stdio.h>
#include <stdlib.h>

int main(void)
  {
  void demo(FILE *fpointer);
  FILE *fpoint;

  fpoint = fopen("data_store","w");
  demo(fpoint);
  /* statements */
  exit(EXIT_SUCCESS);
  }

void demo(FILE *fpointer)
  {
  /* statements */
  return;
  }
```

14.7 Random access

All the functions discussed so far have been used to either write to a file or to read from one in a sequential manner. The data has been accessed sequentially, that is, one character after another. All data in every file is stored sequentially but this does not mean that it has to be accessed sequentially. There are functions which can be used to provide random access to data files.

The most useful of the random access functions are rewind, ftell and fseek. The function rewind is a void function which does not return a value. It resets the current position to the start of a file so that the next character accessed will be the first character in the file. A rewind is done automatically when a file is opened in read mode.

The general form of rewind is

```
  rewind(file_pointer)
```

The function ftell returns a long integer value which indicates its position within a file, with respect to the beginning of the file.

The general form of ftell is

```
  position = ftell(file_pointer)
```

The function fseek is used to move from the current position to a another position within a file.

The general form of fseek is

```
n = fseek(file_pointer, offset, mode)
```

The function seek returns a non-zero value for an improper request. It takes a long integer argument for the offset from the current file position. The mode passed to fseek is an integer which tells the function what reference point to use when moving the position around the file. The following symbolic constants can be used for mode

Name	Value	Meaning
SEEK_SET	0	count in bytes from the beginning of the file
SEEK_CUR	1	count relative to the current position
SEEK_END	2	count relative to the end of the file

When SEEK_CUR is used both positive and negative values for offset can identify bytes within the file but when SEEK_END is used only negative values for offset can identify bytes within the file. It is a good idea to measure the position with respect to the beginning of a file. First use rewind or fseek to move the position to the beginning of a file and then move the position to the desired offset within the file, with respect to the beginning of the file. This can be achieved with the following code which first rewinds to the beginning of the file and then move the position 50 bytes forward.

```
rewind(fpoint);
fseek(fpoint, 50L, SEEK_CUR);
```

The program phone is a very simple demonstration of the use of the random access functions. This program has no error checking whatsoever but it does illustrate the use of the functions fopen, fclose, fseek, rewind and ftell.

```
/*
 * file name: phone
 * demonstrate random access
 */

#include <stdio.h>
#include <stdlib.h>

int main(void)
  {
  FILE *fpoint;
```

```
char answer;
long offset = 0L;
static char array[40];

fpoint = fopen("phonecall", "w");
fprintf(fpoint, "Gordon 853538\n");
fprintf(fpoint, "Ashley 811284\n");
fclose(fpoint);
printf("Display which record (1 or 2) : ");
answer = getchar();
if (answer != '1') offset = 14;
fpoint = fopen("phonecall", "r");
fseek(fpoint, 0L, SEEK_END);
printf("file size = %ld bytes\n", ftell(fpoint));
printf("offset = %ld bytes\n", offset);
rewind(fpoint);
fseek(fpoint, offset, SEEK_SET);
fgets(array, 14, fpoint);
printf("data stored = %s\n", array);
fclose(fpoint);
exit(EXIT_SUCCESS);
}
```

15

Redirection

15.1 Redirected input and output

Normally, input comes from the keyboard and output goes to the VDU screen but it is possible to redirect the input to a program so that data comes in from some other device, such as the RS232 port or a disk file, and to redirect the output produced by a program to some other device, such as a printer or a disk file.

15.2 Output redirection

To demonstrate output redirection compile and link the program repeat. This program normally echoes a string of arguments typed after the application file name onto the VDU screen.

```
/*
 * file name: repeat
 * use to demonstrate redirection
 */

#include <stdio.h>
#include <stdlib.h>

int main(int argc,char *argv[])
  {
  register int loop;

  if (argc < 2) exit(EXIT_FAILURE);
  for (loop=1; loop < argc; loop++)
    {
```

```
    printf(" %s", argv[loop]);
    }
printf("\n");
exit(EXIT_SUCCESS);
}
```

To redirect the display produced by the program repeat into a file called my_file in the currently selected directory run the program from the command line prompt by typing

```
repeat time flys like an arrow > my_file
```

or by double clicking on a obey file (batch file) containing the above command. Creating a suitable obey file is described in chapter two.

There should be only one space between all the elements in a redirection command or it will not be recognized as one. The full RISC OS output redirection command

```
{ > my_file }
```

or its more commonly used abbreviated version

```
> my_file
```

tells the operating system to send the string "time flys like an arrow" to the file called my_file rather than to the VDU screen.

The output redirection command tells the operating system to create a file if it does not exist or, if it does exist, to overwrite the existing file. Output redirection is only effective while the program is running. When the program stops the VDU screen becomes the standard output device once again. The example described above creates a text file called my_file and you can examine the contents of my_file using EDIT.

The output append symbol, >>, can be used if you want to append the results to an existing file rather than overwrite the existing file. For example, type the following redirection command

```
repeat fruit flies like a banana >> my_file
```

This causes the output generated by the program repeat to be appended to the file my_file. If the file my_file does not exist then it will be created.

The display produced by a program can also be redirected to a printer. The device name used by RISC OS for the printer is printer: and to redirect the output of the program repeat to the printer run the program from the command line by typing

```
repeat print this string > printer:
```

The following devices are suitable for output redirection using the Archimedes RISC OS. If you use a different operating system then consult your operating system manual.

Name	Device
vdu:	the screen
rawvdu:	the screen, via VDU drivers
serial:	the serial port
printer:	the printer
printer#serial:	the serial printer
printer#parallel:	the parallel printer
netprint:	network printer driver
null:	null device, no output

It is possible to open a file to any of the standard devices using the function fopen. Data can then be written to this file in just the same way as it is written to any other file. This can give very precise control over devices like the printer if the formatted output functions are used to write to the device. The most useful functions to use for writing to the printer as a file are the functions fprintf, fputs and fputc. These functions are described in chapter 14 and their use in the present context is demonstrated in the program printer. The text written to a null device will just disappear never to be seen again.

```
/*
 * file name: printer
 * demonstrate printing to standard devices
 */

#include <stdio.h>
#include <stdlib.h>

int main(void)
  {
  FILE *stdprn, *nowhere;

  stdprn = fopen("printer:", "w");
  nowhere = fopen("null:", "w");
  puts("Text to screen only");
  fputs("Text to printer only", stdprn);
  fprintf(stdout, "Text to screen only\n");
  fputs("Text to null device only", nowhere);
  fclose(stdprn);
```

```
fclose(nowhere);
exit(EXIT_SUCCESS);
}
```

15.3 Input redirection

As well as the output redirection symbols > and >> there is an input redirection
symbol <. To demonstrate input redirection use the program repeat to write a short
message to a data file with, For example

```
repeat time flys like an arrow > my_file
repeat fruit flies like a banana >> my_file
```

The text stored in the file my_file can now be read using the program display with
input redirection.

```
/*
 * file name: display
 * demonstrate input redirection
 */

#include <stdio.h>
#include <stdlib.h>

#if !defined(TRUE)
  #define TRUE 1
#endif

int main(void)
  {
  char message[100];
  while(TRUE)
    {
    gets(message);
    if (feof(stdin)) break;
    puts(message);
    }
  exit(EXIT_SUCCESS);
  }
```

Run the program input by typing

```
display < my_file
```

Input redirection is only effective during the running of the program. When the program stops the keyboard becomes the standard input device once again. It was suggested in chapter six that scanf should only be used with machine formatted input. Using input redirection is a crude way of providing scanf with machine formatted input.

The following devices are suitable for input redirection using the Archimedes RISC OS.

Name	*Device*
kbd:	the keyboard, a line at a time
rawkbd:	the keyboard, a character at a time
serial:	the serial port
null:	the null device, effectively no input

Files can be opened to any of the above devices using the function fopen and then any of the formatted input functions can read these devices as files. It does not make much sense to open an input file from the null device but it can be quite useful to use the serial port as an input file.

15.4 Input and output redirection

You can run a program with both input and output redirection. For example, the command

```
my_program < my_data > my_results
```

runs the program my_program redirecting the input from the file my_data and redirecting the output to the file my_results.

Appendix 1

The precedence of operators

The precedence of an operator establishes its priority relative to all the other operators. In an expression with multiple operators, the operator with the highest precedence is used before an operator with a lower precedence. In an expression with multiple operators of the same precedence, the operators are evaluated according to their associativity. This means that evaluation is normally from left to right except for unary operators, the ?: operator (used in conditional expressions) and for the assignment operators which associate from right to left.

Precedence	Operator	Associativity	Type
			Primary
15	()	L-R	parentheses
	[]	L-R	subscript
	->	L-R	structure membership
	.	L-R	structure period
			Unary
14	!	R-L	logical NOT
	~	R-L	bitwise NOT
	++	R-L	increment
	--	R-L	decrement
	+	R-L	plus (positive)
	-	R-L	minus (negative)
	(type)	R-L	cast
	*	R-L	indirection
	&	R-L	address
	sizeof	R-L	size of
			Arithmetic
13	*	L-R	multiply
	/	L-R	divide
	%	L-R	integer remainder
			Arithmetic
12	+	L-R	add
	-	L-R	subtract

Precedence	Operator	Associativity	Type
			Bitwise
11	>	L-R	right shift
	<	. L-R	left shift
			Relational
10	>	L-R	greater than
	>=	L-R	greater than or equal to
	<	L-R	less than
	<=	L-R	less than or equal to
			Equality
9	==	L-R	equal to
	!=	L-R	not equal to
			Bitwise
8	&	L-R	AND
			Bitwise
7	^	L-R	Exclusive OR, XOR
			Bitwise
6	|	L-R	inclusive OR
			Logical
5	&&	L-R	AND
			Logical
4	||	L-R	OR
			Conditional
3	?:	R-L	then else (shorthand version)
			Assignment
2	=	R-L	assign
	+=	R-L	add assign
	-=	R-L	subtract assign
	*=	R-L	multiply assign
	/=	R-L	divide assign
	%=	R-L	remainder assign
	>=	R-L	bitwise right shift assign

Precedence	*Operator*	*Associativity*	*Type*
	<=	R-L	bitwise left shift assign
	&=	R-L	bitwise AND assign
	^=	R-L	bitwise XOR assign
	|=	R-L	bitwise inclusive OR assign
1	,	L-R	Comma

The precedence of operators can be controlled using parentheses. Because parentheses are in the group with the highest precedence they can be used to raise the precedence of any of the other operators in an expression.

Appendix 2

printf, fprintf and sprintf

`printf(control_string, arguments)` is used to print to the standard output file, stdout.

`fprintf(file_pointer, control_string, arguments)` is used to print to a file pointed to by file_pointer.

`sprintf(address, control_string, arguments)` is used to print to memory.

Conversion specifiers

Identifier	Format
%d	decimal integer
%i	decimal integer
%c	single character
%s	character string
%f	floating point or double, decimal notation
%e or %E	floating point or double, exponential notation
%g or %G	%e, %E or %f, whichever is shorter
%u	decimal integer converted to unsigned integer
%o	octal integer, without leading zero
%x or %X	hexadecimal integer, without leading 0x or 0X
%p	pointer, hexadecimal address
%n	number of characters printed so far
%%	print the % character

The printf conversion specifiers use the following general form

`% [flags] [field_width] [.precision] [modifier] character`

Flags

Flag	Meaning
-	left justification
+	+ or - prefix
0	pad numbers with zeros
#	octal and hexadecimal prefix

Modifiers

Modifier	Meaning
h	short or unsigned short
l	long or unsigned long
L	long double

Escape sequences

Escape sequence	Meaning
\a	bell
\b	backspace
\f	form feed
n	line feed
\r	carriage return
\t	horizontal tab
\v	vertical tab
\\	backslash
\'	single quote
\''	double quote
\0	null character (ASCII 0)
\xhh	hexadecimal character represented by hh
\ooo	octal character represented by ooo

Appendix 3

scanf(), fscanf() and sscanf()

scanf(control_string, arguments) is used to scan from the standard input file, stdin.

fscanf(file_pointer, control_string, arguments) is used to scan from a file pointed to by file_pointer.

sscanf(address, control_string, arguments) is used to scan from memory.

Conversion specifiers

Identifier	Format
%d	integer, decimal notation
%i	integer in decimal, octal or hexadecimal notation
%c	character sequence, length determined by precision
%s	character sequence excluding white space characters
%f	floating point, decimal notation
%e	floating point, exponential notation
%g	floating point, either notation
%u	unsigned integer, decimal notation
%o	unsigned octal integer, without 0 prefix
%x	unsigned hexadecimal integer, without 0x prefix
%p	a hexadecimal address to be stored in a pointer
%n	number of characters read so far
%[...]	accept only the characters represented by ...
%[^...]	accept any characters except those represented by ...

The scanf() conversion specifiers use the following general form

% [*] [number] [modifier] character

Modifiers

Modifier	Meaning
l	long or unsigned long
L	long double
h	short or unsigned short

Appendix 4

The ANSI standard library

The standard library defined by ANSI is described in this appendix. All implementations of C also provide a non-standard library which defines a number of hardware specific functions. The names of the files in the standard library are always included in programs with angled brackets. Both the standard and non-standard libraries are described in more detail in the manuals supplied with your C compiler.

<assert.h>

This file defines the macro instruction assert which, if it returns zero, prints an error message and calls the abort() function.

<ctype.h>

Defines several functions for testing and mapping characters. All the functions take an unsigned integer argument and return the result true or false.

<errno.h>

Defines the macro errno and the symbolic constants ERANGE, EDOM and ESIGNUM. The macro errno is assigned the value ERANGE in the case of a range error, EDOM in the case of a domain error or ESIGNUM in the case of an unrecognised signal.

<float.h>

Defines a set of symbolic constants which are used to define the limits of computations on floating point numbers.

<limits.h>

Defines a set of symbolic constants which are used to define the limits of computations on non floating point numbers. These numbers are known as integral types.

<locale.h>

Defines the national characteristics including day-month-year (UK) and month-day-year (USA), time formatting, monetary formatting and so on.

<math.h>

Defines the symbolic constant HUGE_VAL and 22 mathematical functions which include trigonometric and logarithmic functions as well as square root and so on. All mathematical functions accept arguments of type double and return results of type double.

<setjmp.h>

Defines two functions, setjmp() and longjmp(), which are used to bypass normal function call and return discipline. It also defines the structure jmp_buf required by these functions.

<signal.h>

Defines two functions, several symbolic constants and declares a data type, sig_atomic_t. These are used to handle signals such as interrupts or abnormal conditions reported during program execution.

<stdarg.h>

Defines the macros and declares a data type required to deal with variable length argument lists.

<stddef.h>

Defines a macro for calculating the offset of fields within a structure. It also defines the symbolic constant NULL and declares the three data types size_t, ptrdiff_t and wchar_t which are the types returned by sizeof, the difference of two addresses, and the members of an extended character set respectively.

<stdio.h>

Defines the functions and macros used for input and output, and declares the data types FILE and fpos_t.

<stdlib.h>

Declares four data types and defines the string conversion functions, the memory allocation functions and a number of other functions including abort(), exit() and system().

<string.h>

Declares a data type and defines several functions and a macro useful for manipulating character arrays and other objects treated as character arrays.

<time.h>

Declares four data types and defines two macros and several functions to read and display the time and date.

Appendix 5

The ASCII character set

Name	Character	Binary	Octal	Decimal	Hexadecimal	Escape	
NUL	CTRL @	00000000	00	0	0x00	\0	
SOH	CTRL A	00000001	01	1	0x01	\001	\x01
STX	CTRL B	00000010	02	2	0x02	\002	\x02
ETX	CTRL C	00000011	03	3	0x03	\003	\x03
EOT	CTRL D	00000100	04	4	0x04	\004	\x04
ENQ	CTRL E	00000101	05	5	0x05	\005	\x05
ACK	CTRL F	00000110	06	6	0x06	\006	\x06
BEL	CTRL G	00000111	07	7	0x07	\a	
BS	CTRL H	00001000	010	8	0x08	\b	
HT	CTRL I	00001001	011	9	0x09	\t	
LF	CTRL J	00001010	012	10	0x0A	\n	
VT	CTRL K	00001011	013	11	0x0B	\v	
FF	CTRL L	00001100	014	12	0x0C	\f	
CR	CTRL M	00001101	015	13	0x0D	\r	
SO	CTRL N	00001110	016	14	0x0E	\016	\x0E
SI	CTRL O	00001111	017	15	0x0F	\017	\x0F
DLE	CTRL P	00010000	020	16	0x10	\020	\x10
DC1	CTRL Q	00010001	021	17	0x11	\021	\x11
DC2	CTRL R	00010010	022	18	0x12	\022	\x12
DC3	CTRL S	00010011	023	19	0x13	\023	\x13
DC4	CTRL T	00010100	024	20	0x14	\024	\x14
NAK	CTRL U	00010101	025	21	0x15	\025	\x15
SYN	CTRL V	00010110	026	22	0x16	\026	\x16
ETB	CTRL W	00010111	027	23	0x17	\027	\x17
CAN	CTRL X	00011000	030	24	0x18	\030	\x18
EM	CTRL Y	00011001	031	25	0x19	\031	\x19
SUB	CTRL Z	00011010	032	26	0x1A	\032	\x1A
ESC	CTRL [	00011011	033	27	0x1B	\033	\x1B
FS	CTRL \	00011100	034	28	0x1C	\034	\x1C
GS	CTRL]	00011101	035	29	0x1D	\035	\x1D
RS	CTRL ^	00011110	036	30	0x1E	\036	\x1E
US	CTRL _	00011111	037	31	0x1F	\037	\x1F
SPC	space	00100000	040	32	0x20	\040	\x20
	!	00100001	041	33	0x21	\041	\x21
	''	00100010	042	34	0x22	\''	

Name	Character	Binary	Octal	Decimal	Hexadecimal	Escape	
	#	00100011	043	35	0x23	\043	\x23
	$	00100100	044	36	0x24	\044	\x24
	%	00100101	045	37	0x25	\045	\x25
	&	00100110	046	38	0x26	\046	\x25
	'	00100111	047	39	0x27	\'	
	(	00101000	050	40	0x28	\050	\x28
	)	00101001	051	41	0x29	\051	\x29
	*	00101010	052	42	0x2A	\052	\x2A
	+	00101011	053	43	0x2B	\053	\x2B
	,	00101100	054	44	0x2C	\054	\x2C
	-	00101101	055	45	0x2D	\055	\x2D
	.	00101110	056	46	0x2E	\056	\x2E
	/	00101111	057	47	0x2F	\057	\x2F
	0	00110000	060	48	0x30	\060	\x30
	1	00110001	061	49	0x31	\061	\x31
	2	00110010	062	50	0x32	\062	\x32
	3	00110011	063	51	0x33	\063	\x33
	4	00110100	064	52	0x34	\064	\x34
	5	00110101	065	53	0x35	\065	\x35
	6	00110110	066	54	0x36	\066	\x36
	7	00110111	067	55	0x37	\067	\x37
	8	00111000	070	56	0x38	\070	\x38
	9	00111001	071	57	0x39	\071	\x39
	:	00111010	072	58	0x3A	\072	\x3A
	;	00111011	073	59	0x3B	\073	\x3B
	<	00111100	074	60	0x3C	\074	\x3C
	=	00111101	075	61	0x3D	\075	\x3C
	>	00111110	076	62	0x3E	\076	\x3D
	?	00111111	077	63	0x3F	\077	\x3E
	@	01000000	0100	64	0x40	\100	\x40
	A	01000001	0101	65	0x41	\101	\x41
	B	01000010	0102	66	0x42	\102	\x42
	C	01000011	0103	67	0x43	\103	\x43
	D	01000100	0104	68	0x44	\104	\x44
	E	01000101	0105	69	0x45	\105	\x45
	F	01000110	0106	70	0x46	\106	\x46
	G	01000111	0107	71	0x47	\107	\x47
	H	01001000	0110	72	0x48	\110	\x48
	I	01001001	0111	73	0x49	\111	\x49
	J	01001010	0112	74	0x4A	\112	\x4A
	K	01001011	0113	75	0x4B	\113	\x4B

Name	Character	Binary	Octal	Decimal	Hexadecimal	Escape	
	L	01001100	0114	76	0x4C	\114	\x4C
	M	01001101	0115	77	0x4D	\115	\x4D
	N	01001110	0116	78	0x4E	\116	\x4E
	O	01001111	0117	79	0x4F	\117	\x4F
	P	01010000	0120	80	0x50	\120	\x50
	Q	01010001	0121	81	0x51	\121	\x51
	R	01010010	0122	82	0x52	\122	\x52
	S	01010011	0123	83	0x53	\123	\x53
	T	01010100	0124	84	0x54	\124	\x54
	U	01010101	0125	85	0x55	\125	\x55
	V	01010110	0126	86	0x56	\126	\x56
	W	01010111	0127	87	0x57	\127	\x57
	X	01011000	0120	88	0x58	\130	\x58
	Y	01011001	0131	89	0x59	\130	\x59
	Z	01011010	0132	90	0x5A	\132	\x5A
	[	01011011	0133	91	0x5B	\133	\x5B
	\	01011100	0134	92	0x5C	\\	
	]	01011101	0135	93	0x5D	\135	\x5D
	^	01011110	0136	94	0x5E	\136	\x5E
	_	01011111	0137	95	0x5F	\137	\x5F
	`	01100000	0140	96	0x60	\140	\x60
	a	01100001	0141	97	0x61	\141	\x61
	b	01100010	0142	98	0x62	\142	\x62
	c	01100011	0143	99	0x63	\143	\x63
	d	01100100	0144	100	0x64	\144	\x64
	e	01100101	0145	101	0x65	\145	\x65
	f	01100110	0146	102	0x66	\146	\x66
	g	01100111	0147	103	0x67	\147	\x67
	h	01101000	0150	104	0x68	\150	\x68
	i	01101001	0151	105	0x69	\151	\x69
	j	01101010	0152	106	0x6A	\152	\x6A
	k	01101011	0153	107	0x6B	\153	\x6B
	l	01101100	0154	108	0x6C	\154	\x6C
	m	01101101	0155	109	0x6D	\155	\x6D
	n	01101110	0156	110	0x6E	\156	\x6E
	o	01101111	0157	111	0x6F	\157	\x6F
	p	01110000	0160	112	0x70	\150	\x70
	q	01110001	0161	113	0x71	\161	\x71
	r	01110010	0162	114	0x72	\162	\x72
	s	01110011	0163	115	0x73	\163	\x73
	t	01110100	0164	116	0x74	\164	\x74

Name	Character	Binary	Octal	Decimal	Hexadecimal	Escape	
	u	01110101	0165	117	0x75	\165	\x75
	v	01110110	0166	118	0x76	\166	\x76
	w	01110111	0167	119	0x77	\167	\x77
	x	01111000	0170	120	0x78	\157	\x78
	y	01111001	0171	121	0x79	\171	\x79
	z	01111010	0172	122	0x7A	\172	\x7A
	{	01111011	0173	123	0x7B	\173	\x7B
	|	01111100	0174	124	0x7C	\174	\x7C
	}	01111101	0175	125	0x7D	\175	\x7D
	~	01111110	0176	126	0x7E	\176	\x7E
DEL	delete	01111111	0177	127	0x7F	\177	\x7F

Appendix 6

ANSI C on the Acorn Archimedes

There are at least two versions of ANSI C available for the Acorn Archimedes range of computers. The current version of Acorn ANSI C is release 3 which can be used on any Acorn Archimedes or A3000 computer with at least 1 megabyte of RAM. Acorn ANSI C is much easier to use on a computer with a hard disk and with two or more megabytes of RAM but it's quite usable on a basic machine with just one floppy disk drive. Release 3 is an excellent compiler but the only user interface is through the command line interpreter or via make files. The first approach is quite hard work for someone used to the Acorn Desktop environment and the second approach is complex and not very flexible. It's very likely that future releases of Acorn C will integrate fully with the Desktop environment and release 3 can be made to integrate with the help of a software package called Desktop C supplied by Silica Software Systems. I have used Acorn C since its first release a few years ago and I must say that release 3 is absolutely transformed by Silica Software Systems' Desktop C. This user interface for release 3 is highly recommended, very easy to use and remarkably inexpensive for such high quality software.

Acorn do not claim a complete correspondence to the ANSI standard but, in fact, the conformity is very good. I only know of two trivial violations of the standard in release 3. There are implementation defined aspects to the compiler which are not specified by the ANSI standard and these are described in the manual in the chapter entitled "Standard implementation definition". If you are going to use Acorn C then you can defer reading this chapter in the manual until you have learnt something about programming in C.

A new competitor for Acorn ANSI C is the Beebug C Development System which can also be used on any Archimedes or A3000 computer with at least 1 megabyte of RAM. I have had the opportunity to use a pre-release version of Beebug C and, although at the time of writing it's still under development, this is clearly a system with a lot of potential. It is a Desktop application and the compiler has the option to work under the ANSI, ISO or Kernighan and Ritchie standards. The Beebug C Development System is not as well documented as Acorn's software, but it's considerably less expensive than Acorn ANSI C.

Useful Addresses

Acorn Computers Ltd
Customer Services
Fulbourn Road
Cherry Hinton
Cambridge
CB1 4JN
England

Beebug Ltd
117 Hatfield Road
St Albans
Herts
AL1 4JS
England

Olivetti/Acorn Canada
160 McNabb Street
Markham
Ontario
Canada
L3R 6G9

Silica Software Systems
Mallards
Lower Hardres
Canterbury
CT4 5NU
England

Bibliography

Acorn Computers Ltd (1989) ANSI C Release 3 User Guide, Acorn Computers Limited, Cambridge, England. ISBN 1 85250 071 9

Acorn Computers Ltd (1989) RISC OS Programmer's Reference Manual, Acorn Computers Limited, Cambridge, England. ISBN 1 85250 060 3

Acorn Computers Ltd (1989) RISC OS Style Guide, Acorn Computers Limited, Cambridge, England. ISBN 1 85250 085 9

Acorn Computers Ltd (1989) RISC OS User Guide, Acorn Computers Limited, Cambridge, England. ISBN 1 85250 070 0

Harbison, S P and Steele, G L, (1984) A C Reference Manual, (second edition). Prentice-Hall, Englewood Cliffs, NJ, USA. ISBN 0 13 109802 0

Kernighan, B W and Ritchie, D M, (1988) The C Programming Language (second edition). Prentice-Hall, Englewood Cliffs, NJ, USA. ISBN 0 13 110362 8

Index